When A Mother's Heart Is Broken

Finding Peace and Joy Through Difficult Times With Your Adult Child

Karen Fisher

Brandon Publishing

Brandon Publishing

Published by
Brandon Publishing
PO Box 1641
Rogue River, Or 97537

Printed in the United States

ISBN 978-0-9966926-0-1
1. Mothers - 2. Family relations – 3. Religious life – 4. Christianity

Dedication

When a Mother's Heart Is Broken

This book is dedicated to
the three extraordinary young men
whose lives had been a struggle
and to their moms who so willingly
allowed me to share their stories.

Acknowledgements

With sincere appreciation, I acknowledge the many family and friends who gave me encouragement and support for the writing of this book.

My special thanks to Barbara Taylor who generously allowed me to share her story with you. Also to the other mother who has chosen to remain anonymous.

Thanks to Denise Haisley for being willing to take the time to read and critique this manuscript. You gave me wonderful insight.

My greatest thanks goes to my amazing husband, Gaylord, who helped in every aspect needed in writing, editing, publishing and marketing of this book and especially for his patience as I reached my goals.

Contents

Preface

They say nothing you will go through in life is harder than losing a child. The loss may not always be a physical death. I have heard it said, and it is true that as moms, "when your children are young, they can step on your toes, but when they grow up, they can step on your heart." I would say, "They can trample your heart."

This is the story of three young men who each had loving parents, above average abilities, and great potential in life, but made choices that changed their lives and the lives of their families forever. Sadly, there are some tragedies, which are irreversible.

What did these families do? Where did they go wrong, or did they? How did these moms cope when the lives of their children spun out of control?

I had always felt confident that I was a good mom. If I raised my children right, they would grow up to be productive and confident adults. What do you do when that doesn't happen? And more importantly, how do we find God's peace and joy through these challenging times when the circumstances do not change and may never change?

There is nothing worse than watching your adult child about to walk off a cliff. It is most difficult when you feel you have tried everything including prayer, and their behavior does not change. You wonder, "Where is God? Why is He not answering my prayers?"

There was a time when I felt the future for our son looked

hopeless. I was praying and trusting God the best I knew how but felt my prayers were not being heard. These situations can drain us spiritually, physically, and emotionally.

The one thing I know for sure is God does not want a parent to suffer and hurt throughout their lives because of their adult child's drama. But how as a mom who loves their child so deeply get the pain to stop?

Problems in life and even tragedies happen to Christians and non-Christians alike. The Bible tells us, "In this world you will have trouble, but take heart! I have overcome the world." (John 16:33b)

Each of us has a journey we embark on in life. Little did I know my journey was about to take me through a time of total despair. It was some time before I realized just how tragic this situation would turn out to be. I was about to cross a dry and dusty desert with no oasis in sight.

I pray the stories of the following three families will give you hope and comfort. When all the circumstances looked hopeless for my family, God was truly only a prayer away.

I share with you practical steps to help you know where to start and how to proceed to find peace and joy. God is ready to heal your heart.

When the word child is used I am mostly referring to "adult child." For privacy reasons some names have been changed in *The End of a Brilliant Life*.

At the end of each chapter are questions for you to consider. I pray you will find answers to those questions within this book.

Part One

Oh My Son,
Oh My Son, My Son

Chapter 1

Our Family's Unexpected Tragedy

I t was 11:00 p.m. when the phone rang. My husband and I were startled. Having five children and three of them boys ages nineteen to twenty-two, who knew what to expect? It was our youngest son, Greg. "Dad, I'm in jail. I think I'm in a lot of trouble."

I could tell from the conversation that Greg was in jail. What could he possibly have done? Maybe he had outstanding traffic tickets he had not paid. What else could it be? But as I listened to more of his dad's side of the conversation, I could tell it had to be a much more serious problem.

He hung up the phone and quietly said, "Greg is in jail. He has been arrested. He says he robbed a bank, and he had a gun." What my husband was saying and what I was hearing were not making any sense. I was not even in shock because what I was hearing was totally illogical.

There was no question in my mind. This was clearly a mistake. Maybe someone had stolen Greg's car and used it in a robbery. There had to be another explanation. Anyone who knew our quiet, well-mannered Greg would know this was definitely a misunderstanding. Our son would never steal anything, much less rob a bank!

This was the one call Greg was allowed to make from jail. We then called back to the police station to get more information.

They assured us that it was Greg—our Greg—who had done this armed robbery!

We were told we could see him the next morning. There was no more sleep that night. I was upset, but I felt no real despair at that point because, of course, we would get this all cleared up.

In my personal journey in life, things were going well. All was good. My husband and I had our life planned. We really *expected* it to go as we had carefully planned. Of course, this was mistake number one. How foolish and naive is that? God had an entirely different plan; one I could never have imagined.

Our children are all close in age, and we are proud of each of them. What a joy they are. We enjoyed watching each of them growing up and becoming responsible young adults. We were thankful.

Our children did well in school and were always very respectful. They were not into drugs or alcohol. What else could a parent want? We had many reasons to be proud.

The next morning, we were at the police station at eight, anxious to see our son. We were taken aside by a policeman working at the county jail. The first thing he said to us was, "Mr. and Mrs. Fisher, your son was in a highly manic state when he was arrested yesterday."

"What do you mean?"

He could tell by the look on our faces we had no clue what this meant. He continued on, "You do know Greg is extremely manic depressive?" We were stunned and speechless. We had no idea where this conversation was going or what he was trying to tell us.

Was he talking about some kind of mental illness? We were dumbfounded what to even say. We have heard words such as schizophrenic, manic depression, and passive-aggressive personality before, but this had never related to our lives and we never gave it much thought.

Regardless of what the officer was saying, I just wanted to see my son. I knew in my heart if Greg really did this, there had to be an explanation. We would get to the bottom of it and bring him home. Maybe it was drugs, or maybe he was hanging out with the wrong crowd, but I knew Greg did not have a mental illness. If there was anything mentally wrong with Greg, I would know. I am his mother.

The officer warned us when we saw Greg he would probably still be in a manic state. He probably would not be sad or scared because he really did not have an understanding of the seriousness of what he had done.

I just wanted to see him. He was my youngest and still my baby, even at nineteen. I had not even shed a tear at this point. I was in such denial. My husband, on the other hand, was not.

When we finally saw Greg, it was exactly as the officer had warned us. He was smiling and not too concerned about his situation. He was a bit embarrassed he had done something so stupid. Other than that, his overall composure was not at all what you would expect. He was talkative, very talkative, maybe too much so. Here we were, talking to our son through a glass barrier.

After about three hours, we found all the facts to be true. We did not have the answer to *why*, but Greg had definitely robbed a bank and used a gun, a toy gun. This was armed robbery and a federal offense.

We were told he probably would be going to prison for a very long time. This was the first time reality began to hit me.

We were definitely looking at a situation that would change our lives forever. Tears and shock did follow.

They say you can always count on taxes and death. This is true. I would like to add you can also count on trials, tribulations, and sometimes, tragedies in life. Tragedy is something that can come into our lives at a moment's notice. It always takes us by surprise because we think tragedy happens to others, certainly not us.

This particular story is not entirely about our son making bad choices, but how some choices we do not get to make in life. For some like Greg, there are choices already made for him at birth.

For instance, if you are born with Down syndrome or without correctly formed limbs, this challenge is something you must overcome in life. Our son, Greg, was born bipolar— manic depressive. He was born with this mental illness, and this illness changed his future, his life, and that of our family.

A Cry for Help

Greg had robbed a bank. He had entered several banks that day trying to build up his courage. Greg is an exceptionally bright young man. However, he robbed this bank without a good plan. He had walked up to the teller, showed her a gun, which was a toy gun, and asked for the money. As he took the money in his left hand, he put his driver's license on the counter with his right hand. (Not the act of a seasoned criminal.)

He had also changed his license plate on his car to a different license plate but also registered in his own name. We were later told these kinds of actions often times are a subconscious cry for help.

Needless to say, by the time Greg was on the freeway, the

police were right behind him. They pulled him over and told him to keep his hands on the steering wheel. They asked him where he was coming from. He knew he had been caught. He told them he was coming from the bank and had a gun on the floor, but it was not real. He had taken approximately $4500.00.

He was placed under arrest and taken to a place he had never been familiar with—the police station. A place where they take mug shots and put you into a cell, locking the door to make sure you, a possibly dangerous person, cannot escape.

If you knew our son, you would never believe he could have done this. Greg was a very easy-going young man. I am not sure where he ever mustered up the courage to rob a bank. I cannot think of one person I know who would have the courage to rob a bank, much less our Greg.

It was time to find a good lawyer. We were from a family who had no criminal background history and had no idea where to start. We were so out of our element, and the obstacles we faced were enormous, insurmountable really. We had a lot to learn about the justice system.

My husband had raised Greg since he was three years old. Greg's biological father and I were divorced; however, he and his wife have always been very close to Greg and very much a part of his life. They, with my husband, and I began our search for the best attorney we could find. Money was no object. Of course, money is always an object, but when it came to our son, we would find the money somewhere.

Thankfully, God led us to the right attorney to guide us. We had our first meeting and I said, "Please tell us frankly what we are up against," and he did just that. He did not sugarcoat Greg's situation and probable outcome. This we appreciated. I am surprised I did not have a stroke right on the spot. Because of the gun, Greg was facing ten to fifteen years in prison.

I was in such shock at that time. No words could possibly explain my feelings. My face must have been ashen. We asked every question we could possibly think of in hopes of getting the lawyer to give us an answer we could accept. But that was not to be. We wanted to know exactly where we stood, and our lawyer wisely took us through the process step by step.

Even though it was a first offense, Greg was still looking at ten to fifteen years in a federal penitentiary. Greg had used a gun, and the charges become extreme when a gun is involved whether it is real or not. The judge has a minimum sentence guideline he *must* follow.

We saw this was going to be a long road, and we desperately needed God's help. Greg was in a particularly bad situation. If he would have robbed a convenient store or a gas station, we would be looking at a state offense. Robbing a bank is a federal offense. We were now looking at a felony and a federal penitentiary. Now that is a word, *penitentiary*, I never thought I would use in the same sentence with a child of mine.

The light had been shining brightly for our son. His future had been filled with great potential and opportunities. Now that light was suddenly dimmed. How did we find ourselves in this place?

It took five days to get Greg out on bail. I could hardly bear the thought of him in jail those five days. Now looking back, how naive I was. This was nothing compared to the time Greg would be facing in prison and what was ahead for him and us in the years to come.

We were surprised at Greg's attitude when he came home. He could not give us a reasonable explanation for what he had done. It did not matter how we approached the subject, his explanations made no sense to us. He had some financial problems, but none that would justify robbing a bank. We considered maybe he had started drinking or maybe he had a new friend and he was under peer pressure.

Questions to Ponder

You may find it helpful to write down your answers as this compels us to answer the questions more thoroughly. In this way we are forcing ourselves to examine our hearts and write down our true feelings.

1. How does a parent emotionally prepare for a sudden family disaster? Would you be prepared spiritually?

2. How does a mom prepare her heart for a child going to prison, a child addicted to drugs, or a disrespectful defiant child?

I lift up my eyes to the hills –
where does my help come from?
My help comes from the Lord,
the Maker of heaven and earth.
(Ps. 121:1-2)

Chapter 2

Mental Illness?
Definitely Not!

The officer from the police station suggested we get Greg to a psychiatrist as soon as possible for evaluation. We found a psychiatrist with a very good reputation. My intention was to clear up this matter of mental illness. Being Greg's mother, I think I would know if he had some kind of mental illness. The fact that Greg had some kind of problem was apparent, but he was definitely not mentally ill.

The psychiatrist we took him to was very thorough. He talked with Greg for a very long time, and many tests were done. It was a good feeling to know we had found a good psychiatrist and were on our way to getting this straightened out. All four parents were in total emotional shock as he proceeded to tell us Greg was seriously manic depressed and very suicidal. What, Suicidal? We saw no signs of suicidal behavior with Greg. In fact, Greg seemed no different to us.

The honesty and bluntness of this doctor was almost more than any of us could handle. We were devastated. He told us without medication; Greg would most likely get worse and not be able to take care of himself in life. My motherly instinct says, "No! No! No!" It does not matter how many times you say this about my son; it is just not true. Greg's biological dad, stepmom, and my husband agreed with me. We knew our boy.

This psychiatrist wisely suggested we see another psychiatrist to confirm his diagnosis. He seemed to understand our difficulty in accepting that our son had such a serious problem. Also, he felt it would be helpful for our case to have two independent psychiatrists agreeing on Greg's state of mind at the time of the robbery. He made an appointment for us with another very well-known and highly regarded psychiatrist.

It is difficult to believe your child has a mental illness when you feel you have a perfectly normal child until they are nineteen years old! We all looked back and none of us ever saw anything that would ever indicate he had this kind of serious problem. He had seemed a little too carefree in his senior year but otherwise, he seemed just fine to all of us who were close to him.

Can you understand why we had a difficult time believing this? Our Greg appeared as normal as any other child. He had a hard time deciding on going to college or not. This was not a concern as many young people are not sure what they plan as careers. We had one son in college. Our other son found himself a good job. We were waiting for Greg to find his way.

I Want a *Different* Diagnosis

Our second psychiatrist did a series of new tests and observations. He took more time with Greg. I was feeling hopeful, and we were anxious to hear the results. My spirits were lifted. I wanted so much to hear a *different* diagnosis.

There had to be a logical explanation of why Greg did what he did. I felt confident this psychiatrist would get to the bottom of what exactly was going on with Greg. After a much more thorough examination, he brought the four of us into his office.

Again to our surprise, the diagnosis was exactly the same! I think no one in the family now doubted this diagnosis except me. They had already begun to accept what I could not.

The psychiatrist asked us how Greg had been acting in the last six months. We had to admit there had been times we did not understand Greg's actions. He was always an excellent student and always received high grades throughout high school. School came easy to him; however, in the last few months of high school he seemed to lose all interest.

Greg's school sent home a note saying he would not graduate with his class if he did not start showing up for classes. He had to turn in a year-end term paper. Trying to get Greg to do this report was almost impossible, even when we explained he would not graduate. It was with great effort on our part that he graduated at all. Looking back, this was really not like Greg. Senioritis is what we called it at the time.

Then off to college. Greg chose to go to the same college as his older brother. After about a month being in college, his brother called, saying, "Mom, I don't know what is wrong with Greg, but he is not going to classes. He sleeps all day. The school has given him warnings, but he just ignores them."

I asked, "Is he staying out all night? Is he drinking? What do you think?"

"No, he just sleeps night and day."

We had many telephone conversations with Greg. All of our talks and warnings did no good. Our excellent A&B student was finally dismissed from college. This was not Greg. We were confused and frustrated with him.

Greg decided to drive home from college, which was about one thousand miles. He did not have a full tank of gas and had only twenty dollars in his pocket. He took off driving home.

This was not our sensible son. Needless to say, he called after a few hours not sure what to do since he had no money and no gas. We could not imagine what he was thinking.

Looking back, we could think of many such incidences. We always thought, "*What is wrong with Greg? Why is he acting this way?*" But mental illness? This never crossed our minds for even a second. Would it yours? There was nothing in his childhood that would give us a hint of mental illness.

Now, of course, in hindsight, we could see there were some problems in the last year. Some of the unusual things he had done were now beginning to make more sense to us. Our answer to this psychiatrist had to be, "Yes, Greg had been having problems, especially with decision making for some time." There were other problems as well, but again mental illness never crossed our minds.

The good thing - if that is even possible, now we have two psychiatrists saying Greg was in a manic state when he robbed the bank. I was hopeful this would help in court. We knew Greg had to pay a price for what he did, and this we could accept. We were just praying for mercy for him. Little did we know his manic-depressive diagnosis was not going to help when he was sentenced.

Prisons are full of men and women with mental and emotional problems. There were serious consequences for what Greg had done. His sentencing would probably be ten to fifteen years in a federal penitentiary whether he was bipolar or not. The word *penitentiary* is still a hard word to say, but in actuality, this is where he would be going—a federal penitentiary.

This was an unimaginable situation we found ourselves in. This was a nightmare. I was scared for him and had no idea how to help him.

After our first visit with our attorney, we came up with many more questions that needed to be answered. Greg had never been in any kind of trouble. He used a toy gun in the robbery. He was young, and it was his first offense. He was diagnosed with a mental illness. He was manic depressive at the time of the robbery.

Surely, the court system is going to have some understanding. Our attorney explained none of the above was going to matter.

A feeling of despair engulfed me. Disbelief washed over me like giant ocean waves—waves of sadness, waves of confusion, and waves of nausea.

I felt like I was suffocating. I could not breathe. I could not think. I was trying hard to hold myself together. I was so fragile each day that I had to take step by step, often moment by moment, trying to calm my emotions. I needed God's mercy. I needed God's grace.

What is Manic Depression?

My biggest question was, "What exact illness does our son have? Where do we start to get him the help he needs?" His psychiatrist began to explain bipolar/manic depression. He gave us the name of several books to read.

My desire to understand this illness consumed me. I read everything I possibly could. Reading about this illness was like walking through a maze such as a cornfield of a thousand acres. It was difficult to begin to understand the complexity of it.

I am certainly not an expert of any kind, but I will explain this illness the best I can in layman's terms.

The brain's function is to filter information to other parts of our body, and the chemistry of the brain influences our behavior.

Bipolar disorder was originally called manic depression, which is a mental disorder that elevates moods and periods of depression. It can cause an inability to handle daily activities as it causes a distorted sense of reality.

The brain has billions of nerve cells (neurons) that communicate to each other and signals messages to our thinking and to our body function. Neurotransmitters transmit signals from one neuron (brain cell) to another. These nerve cells take in information and send out signals to receptors.

Two of these chemicals moving between cells are norepinephrine and serotonin. They are naturally occurring chemicals in the brain, which are responsible for regulating the brain function, moods, and clear thinking.

If a group of neurotransmitters have a malfunction, they will give out too much or too little norepinephrine or serotonin, causing a chemical imbalance.

No one knows exactly what causes this malfunction in the brain, but we do know it begins at birth. Symptoms, however, most often begin to occur in a person's late teens or early twenties although it can start later in life.

Persons afflicted with this illness will have unusual shifts of manic actions and then switch to severe depression. Symptoms can temporarily disappear for months or years and come back again. This makes it even more difficult to diagnosis. These mood swings show themselves in many different ways. Episodes can last days, months, or years and, if not treated, will most likely accelerate.

Manic

When a person is in a manic state, they may have symptoms such as the following:

- Feeling panic or out of control
- Extreme increase in energy
- Euphoria (state of irrational happiness)
- Feeling they can do anything
- Flight of ideas
- Racing thoughts
- Rapid speech
- Do not consider consequences of actions
- Delusions of grandeur

While manic, a person may feel fearless or wired and believe they are capable of great things. Everything makes perfect sense to them and their brain can switch to high gear very quickly.

The manic state leads to behavior and decision making that is not what most people consider normal. Their ability to make good judgments and decisions are greatly impaired as they have a completely different way of reasoning.

Depression

The depression part of manic depression causes emotional pain and despair. The depression is not normal depression as one may feel if they lose a job or a romantic relationship comes to an end. The moods are not just sad but a sense of emptiness, hopelessness, and worthlessness.

Some of the symptoms you may see of this kind of depression are:

- Loss of interest in things they normally enjoy
- A feeling of dullness in life
- Sense of great fatigue
- Obsessive behavior
- Listlessness
- Distortion of thinking
- Critically low energy
- Preoccupied
- Lethargic
- Pessimistic of the future
- Emotional paralysis

This kind of depression is psychologically and emotionally painful. The good news is this bipolar disorder is a treatable illness.

Greg's psychiatrist explained how a person who is manic depressive thinks and acts. He also told us what we could expect in the future years with Greg. He agreed with the first psychiatrist that our son would most likely continue downhill mentally, if we were not able to get him on medication.

Talking with Greg about being manic depressive or having a mental illness was not only difficult but impossible. The connectors in Greg's mind are not working as yours and mine. They are misfiring. A person who is manic depressive has their own logic for everything they do. They do not believe anything is wrong. Greg was no exception.

Manic depression is an illness such as diabetes. A person with diabetes has too high or too low blood sugar. The pancreas does not produce enough insulin for your body, or you may have insulin deficiency. Therefore, this person needs an insulin shot to level out their blood sugar. Those suffering from manic-depression illness have a problem of too much or too little levels of norepinephrine or serotonin.

Thankfully, modern medicine is very effective. Medication can change these levels and stabilize the activity of too much or too little norepinephrine or serotonin. Unfortunately, there is recorded statistics that most people who are manic depressive refuse to take medication because what they are saying and doing makes sense to them.

I have read and been told there are doctors and lawyers who are bipolar-manic depressive and live a normal life at home and work when they stay on their medication.

Greg was born with this illness just as another person may have been born with leukemia or a hole in their heart. This is a chemical imbalance from the day a child is born.

There is such stigma with mental illness. I wish we could open a window on how mental illness is viewed in our country. It would be helpful if it was discussed more in schools or on television so it does not have the mark of shame as it often does.

Denial! Denial! Denial!

I will be the first to admit that I am a hard-headed, stubborn person. I knew Greg needed to be punished for his crime. I could accept this, but I still could not accept he had a mental illness. We have now had two psychiatrists who have given us the same diagnosis. I read books on mental illness, but I was still in denial. I was finding few family members who would agree with me.

It came to me one night. Each psychiatrist who evaluated Greg knew the whole sorted details of robbing a bank. They knew other things about Greg we had shared with them before each visit. I knew before I was ever going to be satisfied and be able to move on, I needed Greg to see just *one more doctor.*

Most people would certainly have given up hope by now for a better answer. Not me. I wanted to find a doctor who agreed with me. I was determined I was right about my son. And so my husband and I with Greg went to see yet another psychiatrist.

We went into the office of the third psychiatrist. He asked what our problem was and we told him how concerned we were about Greg. I said, "We would rather not tell you any details of why we are here but just have you evaluate him." He asked Greg to come into his office while we sat in the waiting room.

After about thirty minutes, we decided to go for a walk assuming Greg would be there at least an hour. We started to leave when the doctor's door opened. He asked us to come in. The three of us were sitting there. The doctor said, "Without going into extensive testing, I would say Greg is very manic depressive and suicidal."

Shocked again? I was shocked, stunned, dazed, and shaken this time!

How could this psychiatrist—without knowing anything about Greg or the bank robbery—in thirty minutes tell us exactly what the other doctors had told us? How is that even possible? From that day forward, I had to stop the denial and see the situation as it really was.

Denial is just being blind to the truth. Some people need more convincing or maybe just *moms* need more convincing. I gained a great respect for psychiatrists that day.

Questions to Ponder

1. Are you or have you been in denial of the seriousness of your adult child's problems?

2. Do you see anger, resentment, insecurity, or mental issues with your son or daughter?

I will say of the Lord,
He is my refuge and my fortress;
my God, in Him will I trust.
(Ps. 91:2)

Chapter 3

What is Worse Than a Ten-to-Fifteen Year Prison Sentence?

When this last psychiatrist agreed with the other doctors, my world collapsed around me. I realized a ten-to-fifteen-year sentence in a federal penitentiary was not the worst thing that could happen to our son.

Being diagnosed with a mental illness, which may or may not get better, is not a ten-or-fifteen-year prison sentence but a life sentence. Mental illness was a world we knew nothing about, and we were in for an unbelievable education.

Let me tell you about Greg. Greg played soccer all through middle school and high school. He was on the high school tennis team and basketball team. He pitched a "no hitter" baseball game. What an exciting day that was! Greg has a great sense of humor. He is interesting and good-looking. He is kind and charming. I sound just like other proud parents bragging about their child but it is all true.

If you were to meet Greg, you would never think anything was wrong. He is bright and intelligent, and he comes across as a confident young man. He seems just fine. In time, however, you notice there is definitely a problem with his judgment and lack of clear thinking.

This mental diagnosis does not change any of the wonderful

things about him. He is not weird or strange. Greg has an illness. Period. His future was so bright and full of realistic dreams. Now... what kind of future was ahead for Greg? How does he adjust? How do we adjust?

This psychiatrist also tried to help us understand what we may be looking at in Greg's future aside from his prison time. All three psychiatrists agreed Greg could get better if we could get him to take medication. However, as I mentioned most people who are manic depressive refuse to take medication.

I felt when I was reading books on bipolar/manic depression they could have put Greg's name in the book. The book explained how this illness starts and exactly what happens. This was exactly our Greg.

The progress Greg's mental illness may take in the future was impossible to believe. For us to believe what the doctor was telling us was too devastating to think about. The anguish I felt and the physical and mental struggle I was going through left me exhausted.

Greg, in this one day and this one moment, made a devastating decision to rob a bank which altered his life forever. All his dreams and ambitions he had for himself were gone.

God knows the reason for this tragedy in our lives. The revelation of this may never be known to us here on earth. This is where faith begins. We had to stop asking *why?* There were no answers. The question is, "How do we handle this tragedy?"

Circle the Wagons

It was time to circle the wagons. We were all going to be there for Greg, and it was time to accept the problem before us. We needed to keep our focus on God regardless of the negative opinions of our attorney and psychiatrists.

I didn't know what was going to happen to Greg. I did not understand why God allowed this to happen, but I know that the God who created the heavens and earth loved Greg.

The Bible tells us to ask boldly for God's help. God already knows our needs before we even ask. In seeking His help, we need to put our needs into words. I had to look beyond the circumstances, beyond the psychiatric reports, beyond the obvious, and believe in the supernatural power of our Lord.

"Ask and it will be given to you; seek and you will find; knock and the door will be opened to you. For everyone who asks receives; he who seeks finds; and to him who knocks, the door will be opened." (Matt. 7:7–8)

We were asking and seeking and knocking. I know we can come directly to God with our needs; however, many times when I prayed, the words would not come. When this happened, I prayed in the spirit. When we pray in the spirit, God gives us a special blessing. He already knows our pain, our suffering, and our discouragements.

When we pray in the spirit, we are saying, "God, I want to be in your presence because there I know I am safe." The Holy Spirit (Comforter) is for each and every one of us. There was no doubt this was going to be a great challenge to face. When I was a child, I was taught whatever trials we must go through, we can depend on God for strength and courage. I felt this was going to require more faith than I had.

The Bible says, "Because you have so little faith, I tell you the truth, if you have faith as small as a mustard seed, you can say to the mountain move from here to there and it will move. Nothing will be impossible for you." (Matt. 17:20) With enough faith, God can move mountains! I now realized how much easier it is to believe He can move other people's mountains. Now it was my mountain, and the mountain looked so big.

I prayed, "God I give you all my frustrations, all my sorrows, my sadness, and my pain. I give it to you, Lord. With the best of my ability, I replace it with the smallest mustard seed of faith I can find deep in my heart." This mountain before us was so high with many obstacles in the way. I prayed that with my mustard seed of faith, God could help us move this mountain.

Not Just a Bump in the Road

This was not *a bump in the road* of my life's journey. This was a gigantic boulder, which had fallen into the middle of my path. This boulder could not be moved by a crane or a bull-dozer. It certainly cannot be moved by us alone. Impossible. I needed God!

In the past, it had always been easy for me to give thanks to God. He has enormously blessed me. Now, however, I felt my life was on the brink of disaster. My heart was in such pain. How do I begin to praise and give thanks in these most terrible of circumstances, my son going to a penitentiary?

I felt my heart had crumpled into a thousand pieces. Remember the childhood rhyme?

Humpty Dumpty sat on a wall
Humpty Dumpty had a great fall
All the King's Horses and all the Kings' Men
Couldn't put Humpty Dumpty back together again.[1]

I felt like Humpty Dumpty. My heart was crushed like a shattered glass bowl. It did not seem possible to glue my shattered heart back together. Because of the continual honest but negative news we were receiving from our attorney, I felt my spirit sinking.

Have you ever wondered what it would be like to step into quicksand? I remember movies years ago where a cowboy is chasing the bad guy who falls into quicksand. The outlaw could struggle and struggle, which would only make him sink further. I had somehow found this happening to me. I was in quicksand, struggling, and I had become so exhausted trying to keep my head above the quicksand. Depression kept pulling me down.

In Psalms, David said God lifted him out of the miry clay and set his feet on a rock so he could have a firm place to stand. Whether it is quicksand or miry clay, I felt I was stuck and was sinking in despair. I could not pull myself out of the quicksand alone. I needed God's help!

Imagine looking at your own young child or grandchild today and thinking this sweet wonderful child would find themselves in a situation such as this. Greg was a perfectly bright and active son who was facing ten to fifteen years in a federal penitentiary. It was surreal.

I knew it was time for spiritual growth in my life. Who do you turn to when the facts are the facts and the circumstances look so grim? What do people do who do not believe in God? Where do you go if you do not know God personally? I cannot imagine facing such a tragedy without knowing Him.

The Battle is the Lord's

This was war. Never underestimate Satan. We called in the troops. We asked everyone we knew to pray. We would put on the armor of God. We will walk around the walls of Jericho.

We will cross the Red Sea. We will push through all Satan's obstacles one giant step at a time. We will overcome!

Greg may end up in prison and his life altered forever, but Satan was not going to steal our son's soul. I claimed, "In the name of Jesus, no evil is going to touch his soul. He belongs to God. He is a child of God."

There were, of course, many days of tears and sometimes weeks of despair, but somehow, I stood my ground. Like a tree planted by the water with roots that grow deep and strong, I shall not be moved. I take no credit for this. God is our refuge and strength. He does not expect us to stand up to Satan alone. He is right beside us.

We have to remember the battle is the Lord's. "Do not be afraid or discouraged because of this vast army, for the battle is not yours, but God's." (2 Chr. 20:15) God expects us to do our part, take our position, and stand firm, but truly, God will fight the battle for us.

Friend, the enemy is real. I do not know what trials you may be going through with your adult child or maybe it's you facing a difficult situation, but Satan is our enemy, and he is very real. The enemy will try to confuse our minds and sidetrack us each and every day. Remember, the battle is not yours to fight when you know the Lord.

What God wants from us is to trust Him and be able to grow spiritually by turning to Him. There are times when things in our lives are out of our control. We can try and try to find a solution, but there is nothing we can do. This is where we begin to grow in our faith in Christ and realize God is in control of all things.

We must put a stop to Satan's discouragement. When I felt Satan was filling my mind with negative thoughts, I cried out,

"In the name of Jesus, get thee behind me, Satan. I will not allow you to fill my mind with fear and defeat."

We have a secret weapon. Did you know that? It is a real secret weapon; the Word of God. We can stand strong on God's Word.

There were times I felt the biggest battle was in my mind. Satan filled my mind with fear. When the enemy attacks, and he will, we must be ready. Through the reading of His Word, God spoke to my heart and gave me strength. "So do not fear for I am with you, do not be dismayed for I am your God. I will strengthen you and help you." (Isa. 41:10)

Whatever is thrown your way can be stopped with the shield of God's Word. We can take shelter in God's loving arms. He is our refuge and our fortress. Put on the armor of God, and be prepared for spiritual battle.

Questions to Ponder

1. Do you feel your heart has been trampled on by your adult child? Do you think they are aware how much they have hurt you?

2. Do you sometimes feel you are fighting your battle alone?

Do not be afraid or discouraged
Because of this vast army,
for the battle is not yours,
but God's. (2 Chr. 20:15)

Chapter 4

The Lion's Den

We have all heard of the things that happen to young men in prisons. Greg being abused sexually was high on my list of fears and understandably so. The stories you hear are very real and not just extreme isolated cases or the fears of an over emotional mother. Sexual attacks, suicides, and murders are not unusual in federal prisons. It was frightening.

I knew Greg was going into the *Lion's Den* without the mental or physical weapons needed. How does a parent even begin to handle the terrible thoughts running through their minds day and night? Satan tried to fill me with fear. He did not give me a moment's peace. He consumed my every waking hour with fear.

Greg was out on bail and at home for many months before sentencing. He was not nearly as upset as we thought he should be. He began working out at a gym and felt confident he could handle himself in prison. This was far from being true. Greg was not street-smart. He was unprepared for prison life.

Faith is the foundation of all my beliefs. There is richness in my heritage. I was taught as a child I could always call on the name of the Lord. When all seems hopeless in life, God is there. Faith is the bridge we need that will take us safely across the river into the loving arms of Christ.

I was raised in what I felt was a very strict upbringing when it came to church, but today; how thankful I am for that upbringing. Some people say religion is just a crutch people lean on when life is hard. Let me tell you, religion is not what we need. A relationship with Jesus Christ is what is needed. He is our direct path to God. Wherever I am, I can at that moment turn to God for help.

I was blessed. I was raised with the strongest Christian foundation, and this is what helped me through some of my most difficult days. What was happening to our son was by far the worst thing that had ever happened to me. A situation I had to face head-on. I had to look deep into my heart to find just how strong my faith was.

I accepted Christ into my heart when I was eight years old. I was old enough to understand God's love for me. I understood Christ died on the cross for my sins. I made the most important decision of my life by asking God to forgive my sins and come into my heart.

From that day on, the building blocks began to form the foundation of who I am. My belief system grew stronger and stronger over the years. I do not take credit for this. I praise God that when I would falter; He has always been there to pick me up.

I was raised with traditional beliefs which included miracles, healing, and answers to prayer. I had never had a testing of my faith like this. I wondered, "Could I stand the test? Could I look to the cross when the circumstances were so bad?" I had to reach down within me and find that strong foundation.

I Will Fix This!

I could not face the thought of Greg being in prison for years when he had been diagnosed with a mental illness. How can this be fair? It is strange how our minds work. I began thinking of every possible way out of this. I seriously thought of going to the White House and chaining myself to a pole until someone would help us. I wanted someone to see how unjust this was.

Leaving the country with Greg seemed reasonable to me. It is amazing how our minds can switch to fantasy ideas. I honestly felt I would take him out of the country rather than have him in a federal prison where he could be molested and killed.

In time, of course, reality sets in. I realized my being a fugitive with Greg was certainly not what God had in mind. Where did my faith go? Was it gone? It seemed my faith fell into a black hole in outer space. It was nowhere to be found.

Moms are always trying to fix things for their children. We want to fill in for God when God does not answer our prayers in the time frame we think He should. Trust God with this terrible situation? No, I continued to try to *fix it* myself. I am sure faith was within me somewhere, but there were times I could not seem to find it, try as I might.

When we, as mothers, see danger facing our children, we react, don't we? If a mama bear thinks her cubs are in danger, she will roar and charge. I am a mama bear. Sheer determination has gotten me through many challenges in my life. I could plow through obstacles. I would fix it.

You can see from my writings that my faith was up and down like a roller coaster. We can think about a problem, try to figure it out several different ways, wondering if this might work or that might work. We can talk to our friends and family getting everyone's opinion. Of course, we can worry. This is what we do best, isn't it?

When we worry, aren't we really saying to God, "I'm not

sure you can handle this, God. I think I better deal with it myself."

Wow! That really hit home with me. It embarrassed me to think this was exactly how I was acting. I was acting like God is not big enough to handle this problem. No matter how much I tried to fix this, it was not going to work this time. There was nothing at all I could do to change the way the court system looked at this crime.

The Useless Act of Worry

Why couldn't I trust God to protect him? Even with my strong foundation, there were times when the circumstances of life became so difficult I could hardly pray at all. I thank God when I did not have the strength to pray, my friends and family were holding me up in prayer.

There were times when I felt every drop of energy was being drained from my body. My spirit was wounded, my faith shaky, and my mind filled with doubt and fear. Have you felt this way before? I needed to keep hope alive within me during these discouraging times. In the midst of problems and crisis, in the midst of my faults and all my failures, and in the midst of my lack of faith, I prayed," Lord, please help me to trust you more."

As I mentioned, worrying is something I am very good at. I have fought this all my life. Of what value is there in worry? None whatsoever. But tell that to a mom whose nineteen-year-old son is going to prison for years.

Shades of Doubt Begin to Sprout!

I was worn down by worry and fear for Greg. This was the time to reach down into my spiritual reservoir. In prayer, I am reminded God is in charge of the universe. God set the stars in place. He makes the sun come up in the east and go down in the west every day. It is amazing; with all that greatness, He cares about me. He cares about my challenges in life, and He cares about my son.

We can continually worry, but this is not going to change our reality. We have to let go of worry, or it will stop us from focusing on God. Just as weeds will choke out crops, worry will choke out our hope, faith, and peace. I asked God to release me from this fear I had for Greg.

I know from my own spiritual trials, you can just say the name Jesus, and He will be there to comfort you. There really is something wonderful in the name of Jesus. As I prayed "in the name of Jesus," God continually renewed my strength.

Whatever your need is today, God is there for you. It is hard when you see your child making bad choices and straying from the things you have taught them. God knows the trials, disappointments, despair, and hurt you are facing.

I knew God had not forsaken me, and He heard my prayers. We do not always understand why things happen as they do. There are things you may go through, which seem so unfair, but our Savior is reaching down to take your hand. Walk with Him. Turn the burden over to Him, and He will carry it for you. When you say the name *Jesus*, He is instantly by your side.

I thought, either my spiritual beliefs all these years are true, or I have spent all my life going to church, singing and praising God and trusting in Him in vain. Have I just been going through the motions, or do I really trust the Lord in all things?

God, Are You Listening?

Does God answer prayer? *I better come up with my answer to this question soon.* Do I believe He hears me? Do I believe He will answer my prayers for mercy for Greg? I thought about this for maybe thirty seconds only. There is no other answer except *yes, I believe!* I have always known God answers prayers.

I will share with you a recent answer to prayer. My husband and I had what is known as a near-death experience.

We live in Oregon where rafting on the river is popular on a hot summer day. He and I have rafted the Rogue River many times and know it well. We know where the white water will be and how easy or hard it will be to navigate through. And, of course, we always wear our life jackets. Until the day we didn't!

We had decided to put our raft in the water farther up the river from where we usually do. As we started out, we didn't have our life jackets on. We were busy getting situated in the raft, with our drinks and food. We were getting our oars in place. It was our usual ritual because we knew we had time to put our life jackets on before the first white water.

This time since we put our raft into the river a different place than usual, Surprise! There was a very long and very difficult white water soon after we put our raft in. We heard noise, looked up from our organizing the raft, and there it was….. fifteen feet ahead of us.

We grabbed for our life jackets, but it was too late. The raft flipped over the moment we hit the white water. While rafting, you need to head your raft into the white water going forward, not sitting sideways in your raft as we were.

We were both shocked to find ourselves in the water in a matter of seconds. I wondered if I would ever come up for air. They tell you to grab for air between the waves, but I never came up between the waves. They tell you lay backward with your feet out in front of you so your head doesn't hit any rocks. News alert! This only works if you have a life jacket on.

In this kind of white water, you are thrown around like a pebble. You are sideways and then upside down. The force of the water was so strong all I did was tumble as if I was in a washing machine.

The reason there is white water is due to the rocks and boulders under the water. My body hit one boulder after another. When a person dies in white water, it is often because their head hits a boulder, and they no longer can fight. My body was being thrashed against the rocks.

I wondered about my husband. Normally, he would be trying to save me, but I knew he was going through what I was.

I fought with every ounce of strength I could to get my head above water to take a gulp of air before being covered by the next wave. I fought furiously. Of course, the minute I hit the water, I began praying.

After what seemed like a very long time, my head came up, and I gasped for air. In hindsight, I would guess my head wasn't above water for more than three seconds. I felt panicked as I couldn't hold my breath any longer and began coughing, which made matters worse.

When I did come up, I realized I needed to get to shore. I tried swimming to shore with every bit of energy I had. I could see the edge of the river, but my body was so beat up and my arms so tired I could hardly struggle anymore.

The shoreline was not an actual shore you could walk up on, but rather a large embankment you would need to climb. When white water hits the shoreline, it actually pushes back into the river as it has no place to go.

With hardly any strength left, I continued trying to swim toward shore, but the reversing water pushed me back. When I fought and couldn't get where I could take a breath, I began to think I may die. Every year, we read of swimmers and rafters dying on the river and often, they are strong young men.

I have heard when a person is facing death, their life flashes in front of them. This happened to me, which only convinced me more that I may die. I was not making any progress getting to the shore. When my strength was almost gone, I prayed again, "God, I can't make it. I'm not going to make it! Help me!"

God answered my prayers. I felt a renewed strength as if God was pushing me toward shore. I felt a strength I didn't have before.

When I was near shore, I grabbed on to a boulder and then slipped off. I grabbed another boulder and slipped off again because of the force of the water. Finally, I was able to hold onto a rock, even as the water was still roaring by. I held onto that rock for a long time before I even attempted to crawl up on shore as I could hardly catch my breath.

I do not know how long I was under water during this whole ordeal, but it was long enough for me to realize I may die.

About that time, I saw my husband rush by me in the water. He still had not made his way to shore. Then I saw him grab onto a rock about twenty feet down from me.

Later, he agreed that he felt there was a chance we may have died that day. A non-believer could say we probably would have made it, if we prayed or not. However, I know differently. I know God heard my prayers because I felt Him near me and giving me the extra strength I needed.

We both eventually pulled ourselves up the bank onto the grass. We probably laid there for fifteen minutes, neither one of us saying anything. We both knew this was a near-death experience. Thank you, God, for sparing our lives!

God answers prayer. When I pray, I feel His presence. When I pray, God speaks to me. I feel him in my heart. I have felt His arms around me, comforting me.

A side note to this is the next day; our bodies were covered with poison oak! We were not just lying in grass but poison oak. We were miserable for days, but that was all right. We were alive!

One day as I was praying for Greg and pouring out my heart, God spoke to me, "Your fears of prison are real, but do you not think I can protect Greg in prison? Do you not believe I can protect Greg in the worst of conditions?" This was not a statement from God. God was looking for an answer from me.

I answered quickly, "Yes, Lord, I believe and trust in you."

Greg is going to prison! What went wrong? It is hard as a parent not to wonder what we did wrong. Did I fail Greg in some way? Every time our pastor preached, I would examine my life. I would search my heart for any sin I needed to ask forgiveness for.

Praise God for his mercy. When I opened myself up to this self-scrutiny, it made me very humble, seeing my own sinful nature. With God's grace, He assured me my sins had nothing to do with what was happening to Greg. God is a just God. He does not punish someone else for our shortcomings. He was not punishing Greg at all. Greg was on his journey as I was on mine.

Still it is hard to not feel you have somehow failed as a mom. I felt my credibility as a good mom was in question. I dedicated my children to the Lord when they were small. I raised Greg to know God and taught him right from wrong. I have prayed for my children continually.

God honors our efforts of raising our children to be responsible adults. We trust they will live for God and follow His ways. We do not always see this happening, but we can have faith we raised them the best we could. I fully trust God with the salvation of all my children.

There were many friends, family members, and prayer chains praying for Greg. We were looking for the heavens to open and the miracle to come. We looked for the miracle, but the circumstances just continued to get worse not better.

Waiting for Greg's court hearing were long and agonizing months. He pleaded guilty as there was so much evidence against him. The idea of prison life and the thought of not seeing him were difficult. The thought of the loneliness a person must feel in prison and mostly the fear Greg himself would have in prison was more than any mom could bear.

There can be long-term consequences for all the foolish choices and decisions we make in life. Greg was about to find this out. Our court date was closing in. We had asked everyone who knew Greg to write letters to the judge asking for leniency. We were begging for mercy from the judge.

I was trying to have faith, but my fear still filled my mind and heart. Where would we find the strength needed to go into this courtroom to find out our son's fate? In prayer, I was reminded this trial before us was small in comparison to God's greatness. We needed mercy and grace for Greg. God is the Giver of mercy and grace.

We prayed God would speak to the judge and he would give our son another chance and not submit him to years in prison. The district attorney saw it differently. His opinion was Greg broke the law, and he needed to pay the penalty, period.

Questions to Ponder

1. Do you wonder if God is hearing your prayers? Have you asked yourself, "What went wrong?"

2. Have you realized that moms can't fix everything?

> *Do not be anxious about anything,*
> *but in everything,*
> *by prayer and petition,*
> *with thanksgiving,*
> *present your requests to God.*
> *And the Peace of God*
> *which transcends all understanding*
> *will guard your hearts and your*
> *minds in Christ Jesus*
> *(Phil. 4:6-7)*

Chapter 5

Against All Odds

Our attorney prepared us for the worst. He reminded us the judge must stay within certain guidelines in sentencing this kind of crime. It seemed so hopeless. From the day Greg robbed the bank to the day of his sentencing was the most unbearable pain for me.

Our attorney was pushing for leniency for Greg for *aberrant behavior*, meaning this was a one time, out-of-character behavior for Greg. It was explained to us that aberrant behavior was a reason for the judge to give the minimum sentence, which was still many years.

It was difficult to see our Greg standing before the judge. He was still my precious baby. Greg was scared. We all were scared. I thought at times my heart was going to stop beating. How did we, a nice Christian family, find ourselves in this place?

In Psalms, David asked God, "Do not withhold your mercy from me, Oh Lord." This is what I was praying. May this judge not withhold mercy. Greg deserved the punishment of the law, but we hoped for mercy.

Finally, our answer to prayer came. God sent us a miracle; the judge was merciful. He agreed this was definitely "aberrant behavior," and we became hopeful he would receive the minimum sentence, possibly eight years. However, the judge did more than that. He made a departure from the sentencing guidelines.

He sentenced Greg to *only* three years in a federal penitentiary. Three years was far less than the minimum sentence he would have received. The judge explained he had never ever made a departure from minimum sentencing, especially where there is a gun involved!

He said, "I do not want to see this young man go to jail where he may not be able to handle the prison environment."

You can only imagine the feeling of happiness and relief that filled our hearts. Praise God, a miracle happened that day! My heart rebounded with joy. The judge gave more mercy than he was basically allowed to do. Thank you, God!

Yes, God answered our prayers. We just experienced a miracle, but this was still a day of tragedy and sadness for our family. This was a *federal offense.*

Greg was to serve his sentence at one of the worst penitentiaries in the United States, Lewisburg Penitentiary in Pennsylvania. This prison housed some of the worst murderers and rapists. They had a designated section intended to house the most violent inmates in the Bureau of Prison.

There were several movies made that were taken from life in this particular penitentiary, such as *Doing Time: Life inside the Big House*[2] and *Dog Day Afternoon.*[3] Some of the inmates who would be familiar names to most of us were John Gotti, boss of the Gambino crime family; Robert Hansen, a serial killer; and Whitney Bulgar, one of the most wanted fugitives.

I think you can only imagine why I was ready to take Greg out of the country. He was an innocent nineteen-year-old and facing three years in a federal penitentiary.

Thankfully, they did not take Greg away that day as I thought they would. They gave him a date to check himself in at the prison. We had two weeks. I had such mixed emotions.

I had joy for this wonderful miracle of only three years, but I still had great sadness and fear.

During these two weeks, our attorney heard some good news. A fellow attorney had mentioned to him he had heard this particular prison, Lewisburg Penitentiary was starting a new program. The program called Intensive Confinement Center (ICC) was a program very much like a military boot camp for prisoners.

They wanted to try separating one hundred men from the rest of the prison population to see if they had a better success rate at rehabilitation. In the program, inmates would be treated differently. They would have educational and vocational training. They had classes on life skills and responsible decision making. They gave them work and exercise programs.

The program was so new our attorney had not heard about it until his fellow attorney mentioned it to him. This had never been done before at this prison.

You can imagine our excitement! I knew this was another answer to our prayers. God had another plan, and this was going to be another miracle. This was definitely God! We told all our wonderful prayer partners the news.

Our attorney proceeded to write a letter on Greg's behalf. I was flying back with Greg to report to the Lewisburg Penitentiary in two weeks. The time was getting closer for us to go. We were leaving on a Sunday, spending the night, and he would turn himself in on Monday.

Faith as Small as a Mustard Seed

On the Thursday before we were to fly to Pennsylvania, we received the bad news. Greg would not be accepted at this ICC

Boot Camp facility because he had used a gun in the robbery. He had to be housed with the main prison population.

After being encouraged hearing about this new program, I was sure this was a miracle sent by God, but this was not to be the case. Our attorney then called a person in a higher government position to try to overturn this. The answer was still no. No, they still would not accept him.

God, I don't understand. Our hope was snuffed out in a moment's time. I remember while talking with the attorney, I felt nauseous. I also felt angry, angry, and angrier. This could not be happening. I am so afraid for him.

Finding a solitary place to pray had become not only a needed time for me but a necessity. I wanted to be alone with God. A few days before I was to take Greg to Lewisburg, Pennsylvania; I was praying and God and I had a long and serious talk.

I am ashamed now to say it, but I told God I would rather He take Greg's life than to see him go to prison. I prayed, "Please, God, take him home to be with you. I am ready for that." I was thinking of myself as well as Greg. I knew each day Greg was in prison, I would feel such anguish for him, wondering what was happening to him. I could not face it. I could not imagine getting up each morning, wondering about his safety.

God again spoke to my heart, "Do you not believe I can protect Greg, even in the worst of prisons?" I had to admit to God, "I want to trust you, but I guess the answer is no." Somehow, I could not find the faith needed. I hated to admit this to God, but of course, He already knew my thoughts and my fears.

This same night after much soul-searching and praying, I stopped pleading and arguing with God. I could not think of any more words to pray, but I was reminded again, "All I needed was *faith as small as a mustard seed.*" After quietly sitting in God's presence, I felt a peace come over me. It was as if God, right that moment, put his arms around me, and the panic disappeared.

When I look up into the sky at night and see the stars twinkling, it is with faith that I believe God created the stars. If He can create our beautiful world, surely, we can trust Him for all our needs. I have to believe God can make a way where there seems to be no way.

One time I was hunting with another of our sons, and we had gone separate ways, planning to meet up later. I enjoyed the hunting as I was spending quality time with him. On this day, however, I became so turned around and confused. I could not find my way back to our meeting place. We had walkie-talkies, and I must have been out of range. I tried to call him, but he never responded.

I tried to backtrack where I had come and tried the walkie-talkie again. Still, he could not hear me. I wandered around for hours. He was also looking for me since I had not met him where we had planned. After hours of being lost, I decided to get off the path I was on and go toward what I thought was a road. Well, that was certainly not a smart idea.

When lost while hunting with a friend, they tell you to shoot your rifle three times, and they will get an idea where you are. I shot my gun. I had wandered so far from where I was supposed to be that my son said later he never heard the shots.

I was becoming a little concerned. It was starting to get dark. I felt comfortable hunting with my son, but I sure did not want to spend the night out in the woods alone. I knew darkness was about an hour away, and he would not find me once it was dark. All I could think of was bears and cougars and I didn't want to be their dinner.

I was not on a path, and I never found the road I was looking for. I came into an area of blackberry bushes. Suddenly, I was in the middle of the blackberry bushes and couldn't go forward or backward. I was looking around, wondering, "How did I get surrounded like this?" I started to panic as I felt completely encircled by these blackberry bushes. I became frantic, thinking there was no way out.

I was praying, "God, help me!" I was a lot more than a little concerned by this time. I was downright scared! Thankfully, after many hours, my son eventually found me. I had wandered clear out of the range of the mountain area we were supposed to be hunting. He could not figure how I could have been so far off course.

I felt there was no way out of those blackberry bushes that night. There was no way of my finding the path again. This made me think of other times in my life when I felt so lost and alone, when challenges came my way and I felt lost in life.

Have you, at times, been in a crisis where you felt there was no way out? You felt like you were surrounded by blackberry bushes and did not know which way to turn? This was certainly how I felt when Greg was going to prison.

However, as I took one step at a time trusting God, He was faithful. Only God can make a way when there seems to be no way. If you reach out to God, he will guide your path and give you direction.

I Choose to Believe

I choose to believe! This is the most important sentence in this story. The night I prayed for God to give me peace; I had to make a conscious decision. I will trust God no matter what happens. I will never forget this experience in my lifetime as it was so real. Deep within my heart, I felt God begin to heal my soul. I made a decision. I chose to believe!

Where I was overwhelmed with grief and despair, I was now overwhelmed with God's love. I felt so close to Him. Greg's future was not looking good. It left such a void in my heart, and it seemed nothing could ever fill that void. The circumstances we were facing did not change and did not warrant peace, but the peace that can only come from God began to fill my heart.

Family can encourage, friends can pray, and neighbors can reach out to us in our need, but it is in that solitary time of prayer God meets us in such an intimate way. It is an important decision for us to make. Do we believe or not? I made the decision. I choose to believe.

The mail came on Saturday. There was a letter postmarked a week earlier from Lewisburg Penitentiary ICC Boot Camp Unit. I assumed it was the explanation of the denial of Greg participating in the program.

I started reading the letter and could not believe what I was reading. The letter stated our son would be accepted into the ICC Boot Camp Unit! The date on this letter was written *before* our attorney talked to the last official who told us no.

What? How could this be? We had been told no again and again. This was Saturday, and our flight was on Sunday.

We were not sure we could contact our attorney on a weekend. We did eventually reach him and asked, "What should we do? Should we call the person whose name is on the letter?" He gave us the best advice. He said, "If it was my son,

I would just go. Do not ask any questions. Take the letter and show the letter at the guard gate." This was just what I did.

Greg and I flew to Lewisburg, Pennsylvania on Sunday. We were worried and afraid of what may happen the next day. Will they accept the letter? That night and the next morning at breakfast, I prayed, "God, not my will but thine be done, but please, God, let things go our way."

The first impression of Lewisburg Penitentiary was about as bad as any prison movie you have ever seen. I am not exaggerating. It was horrible. Guards were up in towers with their guns ready. It was a very old building with high barbed wire fencing. It was exactly as you may see in a gangster movie where the worst prisoners are held. The entrance gate had several guards with guns. No smile of greeting. No chitchat. I guess that would be expected under the circumstances.

We drove up to the guarded entrance and handed them the letter. The guard looked at it for what seemed like a very long time. My heart was pounding. Greg's heart was pounding. The guard told us to follow the road to the right. We would see a building about a quarter of a mile on the left.

We drove in and turned right, and I saw a large white building, which looked like a warehouse. It was the ICC Boot Camp for prisoners! Praise God, so far so good.

We walked into the building, and I could hear my heart beating. We nervously gave them the letter, saying Greg was accepted into the boot camp program. They proceeded to check Greg in and did not question the letter at all. Praise God, we had a *Last Minute Miracle!* It is still amazing to think about. Our prayers were answered at the midnight hour. They signed Greg in, no questions.

Thank you, Jesus! Glory to God! Greg spent his time in

prison in this pristine white building. He never ever stepped foot into the penitentiary's main building. God is still the God of miracles. Our attorney could not explain the letter. He did not need to as we already knew the explanation. This was God.

We had witnessed a wonderful miracle! This was not a miracle we read about in the Bible. This was not a miracle we heard about from friends. This was our very own special miracle. There was no question in our minds who we served— the King of kings, the Lord of lords, and the Almighty God. God's miracle came in His timing, not ours.

It is hard to explain how I felt driving away from the prison. It would be impossible to explain what a mother feels at a time like this. It was truly a wonderful miracle, but I still sobbed and sobbed. To see your son handcuffed and walked through those heavy prison gates was still so unreal to me. Even knowing it was going to happen was nothing compared to seeing them take him away.

No Matter How Hard the Road

Or How Heavy the Load —

Jesus Wants to Carry the Burden for Us!

My whole body was shaking. I have never been able to explain, even to my husband, what the pain felt like leaving Greg there. He was only nineteen.

"God is our refuge and strength, an ever present help in trouble. Therefore, we will not fear though the earth gives way and the mountains fall into the sea, though its waters roar and foam and the mountains quake with their surging." (Ps. 46:1–3)

On the way to the airport, I started thanking God for

answering our prayers. I thought of the night I prayed and talked so honestly with God. He knew I had such little faith at the time, but God also knew my heart.

As I was flying home, I was praying, and I felt God's loving arms around me, holding me close. I began to feel a deep inner peace. There was a silence in my mind, and my heart was at rest.

Praise God! Through this experience, I grew in the Lord, and Greg successfully completed his time at the federal penitentiary boot camp. This tragedy, however, did change our lives and Greg's life forever.

I told Greg his guardian angel was overworked and exhausted and had probably asked God for a transfer to another assignment! There is much more to Greg's story, but it will have to be told at another time.

Questions to Ponder

1. Have you felt lost in life, not knowing which path to take? Do you believe in miracles?

2. Do you have faith the size of a mustard seed? If not, ask God right now to give you the faith you need.

If you have faith the size of a mustard seed,
you can say to this mountain,
move from here to there
and it will move.
Nothing will be impossible for you.
(Matt. 17:20b)

Chapter 6

Victory over Satan

My life had been blessed. However, the road I was traveling on during this tragedy was unbelievably hard. I had a terrible fear for Greg. I do call this a tragedy because it was and still is. It was agony at times. There are trials and temptations in all of our lives, but we can be assured God is greater than any and all trials that come our way.

I have always prayed, "God, whatever it takes in life, keep me close to you. Never let me stray from your presence." I prayed for Greg the same. Greg's eternal life was the most important thing, and I asked God to destroy Satan's attacks on his life.

Don't Mess With Me, Satan!

Satan had attacked me daily. He never let up. I was fighting for Greg not to go to prison (penitentiary). I was getting negative psychological reports, which would throw me into despair.

What Satan does is kick you when you are down. He brings even more stress to you with financial pressure and health problems. If you are a non-believer, you probably do not believe in Satan either. Let me tell you that Satan is real, and the evil of Satan in this world is real.

One day, I had this vivid dream or daydream where I had an actual physical fight with Satan. We were fighting in a boxing ring. I was in my corner, and Satan, in his. See if you can get a mental picture of this.

The bell rang for the third round.

Well, I felt like I had already been fighting Satan for months with his discouraging comments. Satan was making me question if I had been a good mother, and he would remind me of the terrible things that can happen to men in prison.

So the third round, I felt I had enough. I was not going to take it anymore. We met in the middle of the ring, and I came out swinging. I was quick, and I struck with a hard left punch to his ribs and followed with a right. I kept on punching.

Satan was not expecting this, and it jerked him off balance. He almost fell, but he backed up and then came in swinging. He suddenly rushed at me, punching hard, and I got a blow right across the mouth.

Everything went foggy. I was surprised and almost lost my footing. He set his feet and swung a hard blow to my head, but I feinted just in time. He suddenly picked me up and threw me to the ground, but I was fast. I was up on my feet quickly.

Satan started throwing punches, one right after another. I was able to move fast and duck all of them until *smash!* His fist hit my jaw and I hit the floor hard. He had strength for sure and determination.

When I hit the floor, I just rolled and sprang up with fire in my eyes. I had been knocked down before by Satan but I always got back up — always.

Ring - Round three was over.

I went to my corner stool. I tasted the blood from the cut on my mouth, but it didn't hurt all that much. I was catching my breath, and at the same time, I was thinking how angry I was with Satan. He was trying to destroy my son and our family. He was putting so much negative in my mind that I honestly felt I was going to have a nervous breakdown.

Ring! Round four

I said to myself, I have to win this fight against Satan. I was going to win this fight. It wasn't like I had no defenses against him. I had trusted and served God all my life, so I had some leverage. I came out swinging, smashing blow after blow. First, a blow to the side of his head, and then I went for a straight hit to his jaw. He ducked, and I missed.

We both continued swinging until we were in a tight clinch. Satan tried to gouge my eye with his thumb. I crashed down my head against the bridge of his nose and heard a crack. While I was admiring my great smash to his nose, he surprised me with a right, hitting me above my eye. It was a nasty gash.

He landed two wicked punches to my body. Now, being a girl and a lady, I had never been in an actual fist fight. I am small, just 5'2", but I knew I was strong. I was spiritually strong. Satan probably thought I would be an easy win for him.

But I was stronger than I looked because I had faith and was growing in the Lord. I knew God was on my side and giving me the strength I needed. Satan was punching with remarkable speed. *Pow! Pow! Pow!* He almost knocked me out, but it just sent a rage through me. He then tripped me, and I fell backward and almost hit the floor.

He threw a left, and I went under it and hit him with a solid

Victory over Satan

smash to the kidneys. He groaned. I knew that punch had to hurt. I then swung a right into his belly. He doubled over and staggered backward. He sent a blow to the side of my head, and my ear split open. I didn't care. There was pain, but at that point, it didn't matter. I was going to fight to the finish.

Ring! - End of round four.

I was back to my corner exhausted and beat down, and blood was running down into my right eye. My ear was also bleeding. My team, the angels, stopped the bleeding and encouraged me to hang tough.

I have to tell you my body was battered and my ears were ringing, but I felt good looking across the ring at Satan in his corner with a broken nose. I felt angrier than ever for the pain and suffering Satan was causing me and my family.

Ring - Round five.

Satan was big and muscular. He knew every trick there was. He must have renewed his strength also as he came out determined. He hit me solid in my ribs several times, and I gritted my teeth with pain.

I fought back viciously. I got in some solid blows, and Satan buckled to his knees. He almost went down, but he hung on. He swung a left to my head, but I feinted to the right, and I came back with an uppercut, lifting him off the floor.

We wrestled into another clinch, and I looked past him and saw Christ standing there rooting me on. I smashed down with my elbow and hit his already broken nose. I could see the look of pain cross his face and the defeated look in his eyes.

63

I think this was the first time Satan suddenly realized this was a battle he may lose. He then had a dangerous look in his eyes and came at me again. I felt a burst of flame in my head of anger. The rage came from deep within me. I smashed Satan with both hands. I hit with a hard right and then a hook to the body and another smashing right.

Satan started to fall, but before he fell, I held him with my left arm and hit three hard punches with my right fist to his face. This split the skin over his eye. Satan's eyes glazed over, he staggered and fell.

Satan was down, and he was not getting up. He didn't move. He was down for the count and done for. The referee held my hand up in victory! Praise God I won! I won victory over Satan! I fought with all my power and energy given to me by the Lord and defeated Satan. Phew!

Exhaustion! Exhilaration! Elation! Satisfaction! My husband told me I had a crazy and over active imagination. He was right but it felt real good to me!

Back to Reality

This is what we have to do when Satan attacks. We have to fight back, not in a boxing ring, of course. We fight with everything within us, and then we stand firm. We read the Word. We pray. We sing songs of praise. We declare the good works of the Lord. We declare victory over Satan regardless of the circumstances because we are children of the King.

I hope my story will increase your faith in the truth of God's Word. In my humanness, I am as vulnerable as the next person in having doubt. In my walk with God, I surely needed to grow and mature. Today, however, my faith in God has reached a new height, and I have seen the victory over Satan.

I had lived on the mountaintop and felt so blessed. This tragedy took me to the valley, and through the darkness of the valley, I had to learn to seek God's face. There is peace for you today no matter how serious your circumstances. God is a God of mercy and a God of grace.

Jesus said, "If you have faith as small as a mustard seed, you can say to the mountain move from here to there." I wanted to have this faith. The mustard seed is one of the smallest seeds, yet it will grow into a plant ten to fifteen feet tall. It will become one of the largest of all garden plants. It is not just its height that is surprising, but the incredible rate of growth that overtakes other plants. This is how our faith will grow.

I may not have the faith of Billy Graham. I may not have the faith of Mother Theresa. God did not expect this of me. He said, "*Just faith the size of a small mustard seed, Karen, is all I ask of you.*" I realized my faith was small, but it was sufficient. The faith I had was set in concrete.

I know now Satan is wasting his time and energy on me. I am not afraid of his darkness, his wickedness, or his attacks. Again, I take no credit for this mustard seed of faith I had. It was all from God. He is the one who makes us stronger. He is the one who helps us mature as Christians.

This truly was a test of where I stood with the Lord. I was so fragile during that year. This was the time Satan pulled out all the stops. He tried to undermine everything I ever believed. I cried and suffered many days and months through this ordeal, but what I learned about myself was Satan had no hold on me. He never had a chance.

The victory comes daily and comes in many different ways. The victory came in the way of *miracle one* where the judge bent his rules for the first time ever and gave Greg less than the minimum sentence.

Again, we had another miracle when we received the letter saying Greg would be accepted into the ICC Boot Camp program. It was dated before we were told by the highest official that Greg would *not* be accepted.

The greatest miracle, however, is the victory over Satan. Satan was defeated! He had no power in this situation because God was on our side. Satan would like to have destroyed my faith and destroyed our son.

The prayers of others helped so much. I could not even share with my closest friends how deep the hurt was in my soul. Words could not describe it. The prayers of others found their way to the Lord because there were times when I had no strength to pray. Because of their prayers, God reached down for me.

Through this tragedy, I was reminded how much God cares for me, and He understood what I was going through. If you are facing challenges with your adult child, I want to encourage you that God understands. He knows the pain and fear you are facing. He loves and cares for you and your child.

I needed rest and healing. When I came home from leaving Greg at the prison, I felt depleted of energy. We have a beautiful area near our home where you can walk along the river. One day, as I was walking and praying, I saw this cocoon. It was so small but it just caught my eye. I stopped and looked at it for the longest time. I was thinking how wonderful to be safe and secure in that cocoon and never leave it.

It occurred to me this is exactly the way we are in the arms of Jesus. We can feel safe, secure, warm, cozy, comfy, taken care of, no worries, just happiness and contentment. I just spaced out into another world as I looked at that cocoon. Thank God for His love.

Eventually, we must come out of the cocoon. The caterpillar in time matures and will fly away as a beautiful butterfly. Like the butterfly, God continues to be with us as we grow in faith and fly away. It is in God alone we find the peace and rest we need.

What is the cross you are bearing? We each have our own unique challenges in life. When we face difficult situations, this is not the time to fret and worry, but it is a time of testing your faith. When tragedy comes your way, you can cry out to God. When you don't know what to do next or which way to go, this is the time to turn your eyes upward to the Lord. If you reach out to God, he will guide your path and give you direction.

If you are feeling despair with your adult child or you feel at a standstill in your life and want to know God's will, just ask Him. God will lead you, guide you and give you wisdom. Wisdom from above is more than earthly wisdom. The Bible tells us if any man seeks wisdom, they are to ask God who desires to give us wisdom.

There are natural consequences to our choices, however, and God will allow things to happen to us to get our attention. He may allow us to go through difficulties so our faith can grow. What happened to Greg will always be a mystery to me. Why did God allow him to be born with this illness?

You may be thinking the same thing about a problem you are going through. We can search and search for answers to *why*, but we do not know the answers to everything and may never know. God does not allow us to know all the answers. After all He is God, not us. There are some things we will not understand until we get to heaven.

I knew I needed to let go of the past and move toward the future because God had a new and different plan for us and for Greg. We praise God for saving Greg from ten to fifteen years in a high security prison, but we still feel the sadness of it all.

When sadness came to me those years, I would go to the Lord and receive comfort. Just as a mother hen will cover her little ones and keep them safe. God will cover you, keep you safe and give you peace.

Friend, you don't have to be a Christian to cry out to God. If you have not accepted Christ into your heart or if you have not been living for God, He is speaking to you now. He is there for you. He is waiting for you to call on Him.

Most people would think this story would end with "and they lived happily ever after." This is not always the case. Greg is still manic depressive. Why hasn't God healed Greg? I do not know the answer, nor do I question God.

And They Lived Happily Ever After?

Greg still refuses to takes his medication, which has brought many difficult situations into his life and ours.

The intervening years have not been easy, but God has been faithful, and I look forward to the day of God's complete healing for our son

The tragedy, which happened in our next story, was difficult for me as I knew the family well. This young man's mother could never imagine how their family would end up with wounds so deep. It is a very unique and unbelievable story. You could not make up what happened to this next Christian family. It is like a "made for TV" movie.

Questions to Ponder

1. Do you believe Satan is at work in the world?

2. Do you feel Satan has been attacking you and your family? What do you think the best way is to fight off Satan's assaults?

Be self-controlled and alert.
Your enemy the devil prowls around
Like a roaring lion looking for someone
to devour. Resist him, standing firm
in the faith. (1Pet: 5:8-9a)

Part Two

The Word that Shattered My World

Chapter 7

The End of a Brilliant Life

No Mom Expects This!

Beth's son, Jason, had been married for fifteen years with two wonderful children. He was the leader of the music ministry at his church.

Jason began by saying, "Mom, this is one of the hardest things I have ever had to do. I want to tell you something first before I tell anyone else." He paused..... "I am homosexual." Beth really could not believe what she was hearing.

This story is about a family who lost their son in a very different way. They lost him to the homosexual lifestyle and then to death.

Beth and her husband, Tom, started their married life with great hopes and dreams. They had finished seminary and asked God to guide them to the first church they would pastor.

Their other dream was to have a family. When their first son Jason was born, there was the usual excitement in the air. He was beautiful, and they were proud parents. Later, they had another son and daughter.

It was wonderful seeing their children grow up. They enjoyed life serving the Lord, raising their children, and having friends. Life was good. They were all involved in church, school, and community activities.

Their oldest son, Jason, had an unusual talent from an early age. He could sing! Oh, how he could sing! At about eight years old, family and friends began to hear this remarkable voice and comment on how amazing he was at such a young age. He was also blessed with the personality to go with it.

He was an outgoing, not shy by any means, fun-loving kid full of energy. He was asked to sing in the youth choir at church and later asked to sing solos. At school as well, he excelled, and his voice began to be noticed by music teachers.

Not only could he sing, but he had a great ear for music. He began playing different instruments. It is a real gift from God when someone has this ability with no special training. As he grew older, he was asked to lead the choir at church, and eventually, he led the music during church services.

His voice was beautiful. I think the angels stopped to listen when Jason sang. His voice and his personality were a show-stopper, and most important, he loved the Lord.

He also enjoyed music at school and joined the drama class. He had an on-stage presence and confidence, which came natural to him. He loved to act. His parents were very proud of him as they were all of their children.

Jason grew into a big man. He was a very joyful, happy, easy-going, lovable guy who had many friends. People were drawn to him. He began singing at other churches and became well known in the music ministry. His heart was full of God, and he loved singing for the Lord.

He loved acting and pursued that career. He began to get a few parts on TV and in commercials. As many actors learn, however, it can be difficult to support yourself with this kind of work. At the same time, he worked other jobs. Life was exciting for Jason as he was doing exactly what he loved.

Jason enjoyed life even more when he met a certain girl. He

met Cheryl and he knew she was the one. They hit it off immediately and found they had a lot in common. Jason found her to be beautiful inside and out. They fell in love and wedding bells started ringing.

They had a very big wedding as they both had large families and many friends. Jason and Cheryl bought a house and along came two sons. More excitement in the family! Tom and Beth's other children married also and their extended family was growing. They had wonderful family get-togethers.

They seemed to be the All-American Christian family. Tom and Beth were pastoring a church. Jason was leading the worship team at his church. Their other two children, who were now adults, were also living Christian lives. They too were blessed with the talent of singing.

Life was good! Life was grand! Or was it?

What was about to happen in this happy family was unbelievable. It came so fast and in an instant their lives were forever changed. They were totally unaware and totally shocked at what was about to take place.

Jason's Secret Life

The next part of Beth's story will be taken differently by all who read it, depending on your beliefs. Beth is sharing from her personal convictions and what she feels is the correct interpretation of the scriptures.

One day, Jason called Beth to see if she wanted to have lunch as he had something to talk with her about. Of course, she was always happy to have lunch with any of her children. Are we not all happy when our adult children call and want to get together?

Jason could talk nonstop as he was always full of some

exciting story or event. He had such a gregarious personality. This time, however, he was very quiet. He picked her up and did not turn toward the restaurant but drove to the local park. Beth knew he must have something very important to talk about.

It was a beautiful day. The sun was shining through the trees, and there was a lovely pond with ducks. She could tell Jason was nervous.

Jason began by saying, "Mom, this is one of the hardest things I have ever had to do. I want to tell you something first before I tell anyone else." Then he paused..... "I am homosexual."

It is rare for Beth to ever be speechless, but she honestly could not think of a thing to say. Jason had tears in his eyes.

She really could not believe what she was hearing. Jason was a leader at his church. He was married to a beautiful woman for fifteen years. He had two boys. What? This just could not be!

Jason began to tell her his feelings. Beth could see in his eyes such a fear of telling her. He began sharing how he had known he was homosexual since he was in middle school and knew it was wrong. He explained how he had been fighting these feelings for years.

He met Cheryl and really did love her. She was wonderful, and love led to marriage. He strongly felt the homosexual feelings would stop once he was married.

Jason said he knew in his heart at their wedding that this was wrong. It did not feel right, and this was not being fair to Cheryl or himself. He felt, however, his love for Cheryl and his positive actions toward marriage would change these mixed feelings he was having.

As he continued in his music ministry, he prayed continually for a miracle. He questioned his marriage, but at the same time, he knew he loved Cheryl. They started a family, and Jason continued to pray these other desires would stop. They had two beautiful boys, and he adored them. Cheryl was a wonderful wife and mother.

"Mom," he said, "it just will not go away. I have prayed and prayed for God to change me." He began telling her of his struggles. As he was leading music at church, he would look out into the crowd and would find himself attracted to a man sitting in the audience. There was no particular man. It happened again and again, and his thinking became more and more blurred.

He told her of the deep sadness he felt in his heart and the loneliness he felt for years. He loved his two boys who were thirteen and fourteen years old; however, the loneliness and sadness were too much.

He wanted to find some happiness in this life, his years here on earth, with someone he could really love—a man! Beth's mind and heart were racing, but she remained as calm as she could as Jason poured his heart out to her. This was unimaginable.

As a pastor's wife, it was usually easy for her to give advice and comfort, but somehow, she was at a loss for words. She couldn't hold the tears back. She cried, and he cried. Jason was saying how sorry he was to disappoint both she and his dad, but he could not go another day living this lie.

Beth's heart hurt for her now-grown son as he wept. She could see he was in torment and distress. Her entire being was aching for him, but at the same time, she was trying to piece together exactly what he was telling her. This was a totally impossible situation for someone like Jason.

Beth thought Jason may have just felt the need to tell someone. The burden was too heavy for him to carry alone and the secret too difficult to keep. He needed someone to talk with. He was in the ministry, a husband, and father. Surely, nothing was going to change. You could see the anguish on his face.

However, he did not just need to share his feelings. He said he could not go on living in denial. He had fought it for years and felt he needed to change his life completely.

He knew he would have to give up his ministry. He had to tell Cheryl and his two sons. Worst of all, he had to tell his dad. In fact, that was exactly what was going through Beth's mind, "How will I ever tell Tom?"

In Beth's belief of the scriptures, those engaging in homosexual behavior, adultery, premarital sex, and prostitution will not inherit the kingdom of God. Anyone can ask forgiveness for sins, and God forgives; but after forgiveness, you have to turn away from that sin. For Beth, this was the most important thing. To lose his salvation was far worse than telling his dad, telling his wife, or losing his ministry.

I realize the readers of this story may have very different views on being homosexual, but Beth's view was, "It is not only wrong, but a sin." Beth could tell this was not the time to preach at him. He needed her love and support. She put her arms around him as she wanted him to feel her love.

Unconditional Love

Beth felt Jason came to her because he knew she loved him unconditionally. He was afraid this may not be the case with his dad, his siblings, wife, and children.

They talked for hours, and she encouraged him to give

this more thought and talk with a counselor, but Jason was far beyond that. "No" he said, "I cannot go on." As hard as it is to tell his family and as hard as it is to give up his ministry, keeping it a secret any longer was unbearable for him. He was like a pressure cooker ready to explode. It was time.

Jason said he had come to terms with his being homosexual with God. He understood what the Bible says but was putting his trust in God's understanding. He planned to quit the ministry and realized he would not be allowed to be a leader in church music again.

Jason felt he was born this way. He said, "I didn't go out looking for some evil sin to latch onto me when I was in my teens." He was going to church and always loved God. He was not going to turn his back on God. He felt he was definitely a Christian and would continue serving God in some way.

All the emotions came to the surface, and the shocking disbelief almost left Beth paralyzed to the point of not being able to function. She wanted to unwind the day and pretend this conversation never happened. She wished she could turn the clock back to 10 am when he called and asked her to have lunch.

Beth prayed with him, and he took her home. She immediately went into her bedroom and prayed for understanding. She wondered, "How could one word, *homosexual*, traumatize her to this extent.

You would think the first thing she would do was tell Tom, but she could not. It was too hurtful, and she was having a hard time dealing with this herself. She needed to pray and have time to adjust to this news as this was going to be a life changing moment for all the family.

She wondered how his brother and sister were going to

react to this news. They had a strong bond in their family, and she hoped it would hold them together.

While praying, Beth realized she was surprised, but in a way not totally surprised. There was a time when Jason was growing up when she wondered if he had gay feelings. It just crossed her mind for a moment, just a flash, and she immediately put it out of her head as nonsense.

This was years and years ago. The instances were silly things that happened. So insignificant she could no longer remember what they were. I think we moms do have a special intuition of knowing our children in a way others do not.

Jason had been fighting with indecision. Beth had been praying, asking God to speak to Jason's heart. She asked God to bring someone into his life who could make Jason reconsider. We know God hears our prayers and hears our requests, but we do not know God's plan for our child's life.

She also wanted to understand better how Jason could have come to this decision. She had been asking herself, "How did this happen? When did this happen?" Jason's only explanation was these thoughts he had were present from an early age.

Sex is the first thing that comes to your mind when hearing the word homosexual. For Beth, this was too much to think about for even a minute. It was just too awful, too painful, and too unbelievable. She refused to allow herself to think of it.

A week or so later, Beth wanted to have another chance to talk to her son. She asked for God's guidance. They met at a nearby restaurant. She wanted to get Jason to see he was choosing a life of sin, and this lifestyle had many obstacles. It was not going to be easy with all the prejudice against men who are gay.

She wanted him to consider how his life could be destroyed. What will happen to your ministry? What about your family?

They may reject you. Your friends may abandon you. There is no going back once you make this decision.

Until now, Jason had resigned himself to his present life even though he felt empty inside. He loved his wife and adored his children but had come to his final conclusion. He was going to change the direction of his life. He believed he could have this different future and still have God in his life. He prayed he would not lose his son's love.

Beth was feeling truly alone. She was the only one who knew Jason's secret. She wanted to tell her husband but dreaded seeing the pain on his face and the hurt he would feel. Beth could think of nothing else for days—all day, every day and every night.

This news came so unexpected. It was like a flashflood, which comes with no warning. Beth felt she was in the eye of a storm. This was not a natural storm but an emotional storm.

She asked herself, "Is it a mental illness?" She had to admit she really knew nothing about being homosexual or bisexual. There were debates on TV about the rights of gays and lesbians, but she had never paid any attention.

She wanted to give serious thought to how this change came to Jason. As a parent, you spend years teaching your children of God's love. She knew Jason loved God. Beth always felt if we raise our children according to God's Word, they would have the same morals and values we have taught them.

One day, Jason called asking her to pray for him as he was going to tell his wife, Cheryl, the next day. She wanted him to wait so they could talk more about it, but he was ready to move on.

Beth had talked with Jason several times but wanted to have one more serious conversation with him. She asked him to please wait telling Cheryl until they could talk again. He agreed. She felt uneasy because she wasn't sure what his reaction was going to be as she had some blunt questions.

They met the next day at the same park they had originally met. She began by asking, "What about your future? Your future has been so full of promise and hope." But in Jason's mind, the opposite was true.

He explained how discontented he was with his life. He had hopes and dreams which would never be fulfilled if he didn't change the way his life was heading. He said, "Mom, I have a vision of a different kind of life than I have been living."

Beth responded, "Yes, but the way of life you are choosing stirs fear in me. I am frightened for you leaving all that is familiar behind. The difficulties could be so much more than you have considered. You are walking toward a new start in life, stepping out into an unknown world."

"Mom, there is a road I need to travel and see where it takes me. I know I will have days of doubt and apprehension. I am prepared for whatever comes. I will learn to find my way through this new life. I feel I need to escape a boring life, an uneventful life, and a disappointing life. I don't want to look back on my life with regrets."

Beth explained how she and Tom disapproved of the gay lifestyle, but they were not violent people. However, some people feel so strongly against homosexuals, and they *are violent* people and do violent things. You can hear story after story on the news of abuse and harassment of gay men. Homosexuals go through hostility and rejection. People make comments and insults that are hurtful.

Beth said, "I don't understand. You have a good life, but you are willing to leave it all behind. Have you figured the cost before taking this step? Who will stand with you? Will any of your friends still be friends?"

"Of course I have thought of all these things. This was not an easy decision for me. I have always known I was different. I didn't try to be different. I just am." Jason discovered early in life this difference was not accepted by most people.

Beth was surprised as it seemed Jason had a remarkable confidence in what he was doing. He said, "I have had lots of time to think and to plan. I want to discover who I am. Don't I deserve happiness like you and Dad? Like other couples? There is something within me that is seeking deeper love. There has to be something more for me; a place to belong. I hope to not lose the love of my family."

To ask Jason if he had really thought this through was really a foolish question as Jason would never put himself and his family through this without a great deal of thought and prayer. He actually had thought about this for years.

It was uncomfortable for Beth, but she wanted to understand more. She asked him, "How do you go about meeting other homosexuals? I can't imagine you going to bars." Beth could not help wondering if he already had some homosexual friends.

He seemed so calm about it all. Never in her wildest imagination could she consider that she would be asking her son this, but "What about AIDS?" These were extremely sensitive questions.

Jason explained his decision wasn't about sex. It was about the deep desire to have love and affection. He said, "I don't feel I fit or belong anywhere." That comment would surprise anyone who knew Jason because he seemed to be very well liked by everyone who knew him. He was a leader not a follower.

I was thinking about his comment of not belonging, and I realized *everyone liking you* has nothing to do with a person feeling like *they belong.* It is two entirely different things. Jason didn't know if his whole family would turn against him. What would his parents do? What would his boys do? Would they stop loving him?

Even with these questions in mind, he still decided his direction in life had to change. There was nothing to be said to change his mind. He had, obviously, already asked himself all these questions before many times.

Questions to Ponder

1. Do you have unconditional love for your child
    whatever lifestyle he or she chooses?

2. Can you trust God to take care of your child, even
    when you see they are living a life of sin?

Find rest,
O my soul in God alone;
my hope comes from him.
He alone is my rock and my salvation;
He is my fortress, I will not be shaken.
(Ps. 62: 5-6)

Chapter 8

Honey, I'm Home!
(Homosexual)

Jason was leading a life of quiet desperation. He spent the day shaking, weeping, and praying. How was he going to be able to tell Cheryl? He felt sure she had no suspicions, and this would make it doubly hard. The time had come. He chose a night when their boys were gone.

He asked her to come and sit down in the living room so they could talk about something important. First, he told her how much he loved her and what she meant to him. He told her how much he loved their boys. Cheryl was feeling tears start to come.

Later, she said she did not know why she felt tearful because she knew in her heart they had a good marriage. He could have wanted to talk about financial problems, moving to another city, or a whole list of things. There was no reason for her to feel this fear, but something about Jason made her feel this conversation was not going to be good.

She could not imagine he wanted a divorce or had fallen in love with someone else. She would have sensed something wrong. They were together almost all the time, and he was a wonderful loving husband. But actually, this was exactly what he was about to say. He wanted a divorce, but not because he had fallen in love with another woman.

What he said next was beyond belief and beyond anything she could have possibly considered. "Cheryl, this is so hard for me to tell you, but I am homosexual and I want a divorce." She first felt relieved because she knew he was joking. This was her loving husband of 15 years. She knew he had to be kidding.

After smiling for a minute, she looked into his eyes and saw he was not joking. I cannot even presume to know how a man or woman would feel hearing this from their spouse. So many things must have gone through Cheryl's mind. She was in a state of disbelief and could hardly react. What do you say when your husband says this to you?

At first, her mind refused to hear what he was saying because it was just so absurd! Jason shared he was not happy in their marriage even though he loved her. He explained he could not go on another day living this life they had together.

Once she realized this was not a joke, the questions in her mind were coming faster than she was able to speak. "Do you want a divorce because you love some man? Have you been sleeping with men? When you are with me, you are thinking of some man you met, or is it really another woman? Are you trying to hide some adulterous affair with a woman? You are a Christian. How can this be?"

Yes, he did have feelings for men. He explained he had feelings, but he had never acted on any of those feelings. No, he was not seeing a man now and never had up to this time. No, he has not had sex with a man.

Cheryl was asking, "When did this start? How long have you known? Did you know this when you married me? Why haven't you told me before? Who else knows? Don't you believe what the Bible says about being homosexual? Did you ever love me?"

The questions and the explanations went on for hours. She was in disbelief. After many hours of talking, the tears came like a flood. Cheryl doubled over in grief and pain. It was almost like wailing, pleading for this not to be true.

She did not want to know another thing, but at the same time, she could not stop asking questions to try to make some sense of it. Was she having a bad dream? Was this really happening?

When she finally went to bed, all she could think of were more questions. Is Jason telling me the truth? Had he really not slept with a man? Was he seeing some man right now, or was there another woman? Was he really going to quit the ministry and tell this to our church friends? How would they tell their boys? The questions kept coming but with no answers.

What a difficult and desperate situation Cheryl found herself in. The next morning, Cheryl was trying to think of who she could call for support. Do I call my mom? Do I call his mom? No, no. News travels fast. There are some things you do not talk about to anyone.

I would guess a few of you reading this book has had this experience happen to you. I am sure Beth had been praying continually for her daughter-in-law, Cheryl, knowing Jason was going to be telling her. Beth felt her own burden was unbearable. There are times we have to stand back and look at our situation exactly as it is and be able to accept this new reality.

Have you ever found yourself in a dilemma such as this? A situation so bad you felt there was no answer that would ever make sense. A time in your life that the unimaginable happened, and you felt you had nowhere to turn. Who do you turn to? Who do you trust to talk to about something so personal?

There are many different challenges we can see our children

go through. Your child could have a terminal illness, a failed business, or broken relationship. Beth never would have guessed her son being homosexual. She had to be strong for her family and especially for her daughter-in-law, Cheryl.

The cruel reality of what they would be going through is like driving into a brick wall. It stops us dead in our tracks and all the other things happening in our lives become very insignificant.

Beth's daughter-in-law, Cheryl, eventually poured her heart out to her mother-in-law. She was heartbroken.

Beth had no answers for her, but she did know someone they could talk to. A friend they both knew who would understand. That friend was Jesus. Beth and Cheryl began to pray and together ask Jesus for understanding and calm. Many of us know this next hymn, but read the words slowly.

What a friend we have in Jesus
All our sins and grief to bear
What a privilege to carry
Everything to God in prayer.

Oh, what peace we often forfeit
Oh what needless pain we bear
All because we do not carry
Everything to God in prayer.[4]

Jesus knows! He knows our pain and the sorrow we go through. In our humanness, we try to understand, but Jesus is the only one we can turn to. The best Beth could do was to remind Cheryl they have a friend in Jesus.

Like this song says, "Oh, what needless pain we bear, all

because we do not carry everything to God in prayer." Beth and Cheryl asked God to help them carry this heavy burden.

Time to Tell Dad

Beth wanted to really understand this new life Jason was choosing in respect to what the Bible says. She was having trouble processing the whole homosexual lifestyle. It was only when someone in her own family was homosexual that she began to read more and try to comprehend this fully. She felt she owed this to her son.

Beth went to the bookstore to buy books to give her a better understanding. Some of the books were helpful as they were written to help support parents of homosexuals. At the same time, she read other books that were very difficult for her to even read. This was a foreign world to her.

Beth had been crying for days. Every day was filled with anxiety. Tom kept asking her what was wrong, and she told him every reason she could think of except the real reason for her tears. Tom, being a minister, had counseled people about every part of life's challenges, and he was always able to think through any problem a person may bring to him.

However, Beth still could not bring herself to tell him. Jason could not face his dad, so he wrote him a letter and asked Beth to give it to him. One evening, she gave Tom the letter to read, and after reading it, he sat silent and tears welled up in his eyes. You could see he was overwhelmed with grief.

She put her arms around him to comfort him and tried to get him to talk, but he could not. Tom went out for a walk, and when he came home, he went straight to bed.

The next morning, Tom would say again and again, "How did this happen?" The Bible tells us, "Train up a child in the way he should go and when he is old, he will not turn from it." (Prov. 22:6) How could he have not sensed this about Jason?

They felt their world had fallen apart. What do parents do with this kind of information from their son? They could preach at him, put guilt on him, scream at him, but all this would only drive him away.

Because of what we went through with Greg, I now realize that none of us can guess what might happen to our own child when they are adults. Our children are so adorable growing up. On Greg's first Easter I dressed him in a bunny outfit and at Halloween he was dressed as a pumpkin. We show off our children because we are so proud of them, don't we?

Who would guess as adults they may spend time in a federal penitentiary? Who would guess your married son would announce in his thirties that he is homosexual?

You look at your teenage or young adult son or daughter and wonder how did we get from this little darling to the situation we now find ourselves? We raised them in a good environment and taught them the right principles. Tom told Beth, "I now really understand what a broken heart feels like."

God Heals The Broken Hearted Do You Need God's Healing Today?

What went wrong? Tom and Beth never had problems with drugs or alcohol with any of their children. No problems with being promiscuous. Jason was such a happy kid when he was young. He played with the neighbor kids, loved his dog, rode his bike, and played baseball. They had this precious child with priceless memories.

Beth looked through pictures of Jason when he was in first grade and middle school. He was no different than any little boy. The question kept coming back to Tom, "How could Jason be a leader at church for years and not understand he cannot give into this sin? Does he not understand the eternal consequences?" It took Tom months before he and Jason were able to sit down and talk.

Conversation seemed tense and awkward between Jason and his dad. They had always in the past had much to talk about since they were both in the ministry. Tom wondered, "How can you know someone so well and not know a thing like this?"

A Terrible Nightmare!

Cheryl had hoped this whole thing was a terrible nightmare. She wished she could turn back the clock and pretend this never happened, but she knew in her heart, things in her family would never be the same. The pain she was dealing with was beyond difficult, and she hated to think of the pain her two boys were about to go through.

If your children are not doing their chores, you say, "Boys come in the living room and sit down. We need to talk about something." If your child is getting bad grades, you say, "Come sit down at the table, you and I need to talk." How does one bring up this subject with two boys thirteen and fourteen years old?

Jason was going to be moving out. Cheryl wondered, "Will I be raising the boys alone? What involvement will Jason have in his son's lives? Would the boys want him in their lives?" The time had come to tell them.

Jason was sweating, his face beading with perspiration. When he began to talk, his voice could almost not be heard. Jason now knew telling his dad and telling Cheryl was not the hardest thing. Telling his two boys was the hardest thing he would ever have to do.

Jason was able to begin. He told them how unhappy his life was even though he loved them and their mother very much. He told how he never felt he really fit in when he was growing up. He explained how he still loved God very much.

And then... He simply said, "Boys, this is going to be very hard for you to understand, but your mother and I are getting a divorce." This in itself really came as a surprise as their parents always seemed so happy.

The next statement was not just a surprise, but shocking. Jason said, "I am homosexual. I became aware of it when I was about your age, and I have fought it for years. I cannot continue living a lie. I know this will be hard for you to understand, but I am trusting God to help you.

I will always love you. I will always be there for you. I can only pray you will forgive me for hurting you and your mother. I never meant to. Your mom and I will be getting a divorce, and I will be moving out."

Jason did not know how the boys were going to react, but he knew it would not be easy for them. Most of the boy's friends were from their church. How were they going to face their friends?

Both boys were speechless at first. Then, the oldest son, Chad, let loose. He began cussing and swearing at his dad. Cussing was something Chad never did. He asked, "You sleep with men? You want to kiss men? You never loved Mom? You never loved us? You would rather live with some man than with us?"

Cheryl tried to calm Chad, but he was not going to be calmed down. He became enraged and stormed out of the house. Chad did not come home that night or the next.

Justin, the youngest son, said nothing. Not a word. His eyes welled up with tears as Chad was yelling and cussing. He stood up and went to his bedroom almost in a daze. Cheryl decided to leave him alone and give him time to himself.

Later, she heard him up several times during the night. The next morning at breakfast, he stared at his food. She tried to talk to him, but he had nothing to say. He went back to bed and did not go back to school for a week. He was very despondent.

Cheryl worried about Chad but knew he had to let all his anger out. She knew he would come back when he was ready. Chad and Justin had many good friends at church and school. How would they be able to face them? What would the other kids say? Thirteen and fourteen years old are such a vulnerable time for them.

Months went by, and in time, the boys were able to find their footing again. The family was mostly worried about Chad because of his displays of anger and his sliding grades in school. Beth, being grandma, just prayed, "God, we need you beside us. Please let Cheryl and our grandsons feel your love."

It was years later they found out Justin was the one they should have worried about. Justin later said, "He had thoughts of suicide many times rather than face friends at school and church." It is sometimes the quiet child that is having the hardest time.

Chad was angry for a long time and continued to profess his disgust of his dad's new life change. It took about a year before he began to act like himself again. They would forever be affected by what had happen in their family. Cheryl was a rock for them as well as Tom and Beth, their grandparents.

Who Was Jason Really?

The Jason everyone saw for years was not the real Jason. Those who thought they knew him best only knew a side of him. They never knew the secret he had been hiding for years and the grief he was going through.

We tend to look at the outward appearance of others. We can all put on a good face, showing others what we want them to see. Jason did a very good job of putting on the happy face. He was an actor and was probably better than most at just letting friends see him in a certain light.

He could share laughter and fun with his friends and family, but there was great sadness and confusion in his heart and mind, which he could not share. I have wondered what he must have been going through and tried to understand his emotions and feelings during this time. He must have felt very alone.

Jason was feeling uncertain and confused by his teaching of right and wrong. What he was taught as a child was not what he was feeling even at a young age. He was going through spiritual warfare and temptation. Jason put on a mask of happiness and tried to live the life that was expected of him.

Your parents, family, and friends expect you to start dating girls, so he went through the motions of dating. You are expected to get married and have children. As you live the lie, you get better at acting the part. You cannot talk to anyone about your true feelings as you are afraid of rejection. You continue living the life everyone expects of you.

Jason explained to Beth, "One day, I woke up and I knew immediately I was not going to continue living this life of sadness. I know I am a child of God, and I am the same person I have always been." It was at this time he began to wrestle with the thoughts of change. "I feel as if my life is like a puzzle that had pieces missing. I have these other pieces, but try as I might, the pieces don't fit."

It took great courage for him to face the world and share his secret. He had decided to start a new life of which the challenges would be overwhelming. He wanted a new life and a new identity. Even in this situation, he wanted to be of service to the Lord.

It's hard to imagine the courage needed, but Jason told the deacons at his church and resigned from his music ministry. This was difficult as he loved singing for the Lord. The deacons were in disbelief, and he felt their rejection. Jason had been an amazing example of a wonderful Christian leader for years.

He then told a few close friends, and word soon spread like wildfire. No one could believe this! Everyone had this image in their minds of Jason, their musical leader, their strong Christian counselor, and their close friend.

Jason was always a dreamer and always full of new ideas and energy. Everyone thought they knew him, but no one knew the unhappiness he felt in his heart.

Beth wanted to be strong for him. She knew she was the one person Jason knew he could turn to. She also knew she had to accept the life she had imagined for her son was not to be.

Jason made his decision and was now looking forward to a new beginning. He seemed excited to start his new life. The hard part of telling everyone was behind him. He and Cheryl divorced. Everyone had to adjust. His parents, his siblings, his friends, and his children all had to come to terms with how to accept Jason's new lifestyle.

Beth told Tom, "If we want a relationship with our son, we have to find some tolerance and acceptance. We still love him. He is the same son we have known for years and loved."

Tom and Beth did not see Jason as often as before. He was finding his way in this new life he chose. He had found a new job and continued with his acting. It seemed he was cutting all ties with most everyone he knew.

Tom and Beth began to avoid contact with friends as well. It was difficult seeing people they had known for years. Gossip had spread to everyone, and everyone reacted in different ways. They felt uncomfortable around friends and family. It was awkward because they could tell friends did not know what to say to them. Others would avoid them.

Beth knew Jason was living in sin, but she put her trust in God. She felt she could accept and love her gay son without approving his lifestyle. She could not allow herself to think Jason would not have eternity in heaven.

Jason had a heart for God, and he loved the Lord. The Bible tells us David had a heart for God. David did some terrible things in his life, but he always had a heart for God and God honored that.

This was a difficult time for Beth, and because of what I went through with Greg, I could understand her pain.

Who holds us together when we feel lost and everything looks hopeless? These times of despair will bring us to our knees. Beth prayed continually for her son. She would kneel and say, "Here I am again, Lord." The Bible tells us to call on the name of the Lord when going through challenges and hardships, and He will be there.

It was surprising, but in time, Jason found a church who accepted homosexuals. Most people attending the church were not homosexual, but they were open to any and all who wanted to attend. They were also open to homosexuals participating in the services.

Jason became involved in their music ministry. He had no idea when he left his church if he would ever be able to serve

God by singing again. This was a wonderful surprise for him as he never considered it remotely possible he would have this opportunity. He had not known of churches where homosexuals were accepted.

Beth had to admit Jason seemed happier. She wondered how he had the strength needed to *come out of the closet*, so to speak. It had to be a very difficult decision for him. He seemed happy, and she and Tom were fine not asking questions. They would rather not know any more about his new life.

That is easy to say; however, Beth told me, "The truth is, you really want to know what is happening but afraid to ask." They would hear he was "dating" someone, or a family member would say they saw him with someone. Whenever he did stop by, they always talked of other things.

Jason's carefree attitude was difficult for her to grasp. Beth always felt he may have already had gay friends before he talked with her the first time. He was uncomfortable now around most of his previous friends. It took great courage for Jason to start this new life, but you could tell he was happy with his decision.

But then, of course, Jason eventually met a special person in his life, the significant other.

Questions to Ponder

1. Do you feel you are carrying an unbearable burden? Do you sometimes feel you are having a terrible nightmare that you can't wake up from?

2. Is your heart broken and your spirit crushed as you watch your child struggle in life?

The Lord is close to the
brokenhearted
and saves those who
are crushed in spirit.
(Ps. 34:18)

Chapter 9

Meeting the
Significant Other!

In about a year, Jason called and told Beth he had met someone he cared very much for and wanted his dad and her to meet him. This was definitely going to be a tough hurdle. It is one thing to know your son is homosexual. It is another thing to meet someone he cares for and is having sexual relations with.

Beth was never able to allow herself to think of this part of Jason's new life. She had to stop herself from thinking about anything sexual the moment it entered her head. She thanked God that somehow, someway; He helped her to do that.

Tom said, "No, I do not want to meet him. I have come to accept Jason's decision, but I do not care to meet his new *partner* in life." In time, Beth convinced Tom to go. They loved their son, and they were not going to turn away from him. The date was set for them to meet this *new friend.*

Talk about uncomfortable! How could anyone be comfortable in this situation? Parents who are ministers meeting their homosexual son's significant other. All day, Beth wanted to call Jason and cancel. She spent time on her knees, praying everything would go well.

They liked Jonathon, but feelings at the table were still raw. Tom and Beth usually were never at a loss for words; however, this night, they did not know what to say. Nothing about that night went well, but thankfully, they made it through the evening. It was one night. Surely, the second time they were together would be easier.

Beth assumed this was an important person to Jason as he would never put them through this for someone he was just dating. It was interesting to Tom and Beth that Jonathon was a very small man in both statue and weight. It seemed strange to them to see the attraction when you see how very large a man their son was. They were an odd-looking couple. This just proves again that opposites attract.

Jason and Jonathon were together from then on. After a time, Jason's two boys even came around and were able to accept their father's significant other. No one approved of his lifestyle choice, but Jason was still a wonderful son and a good father.

The next holiday get-together was Christmas, and Jason had asked to bring Jonathon. There was a lot of apprehension on the part of his brother and sister and their families. For instance, what do they tell their children why Uncle Jason is not there with their Aunt Cheryl, and who is this man? Jason's two boys decided not to come.

The house was beautiful with the outside lights Tom puts up every year. The Christmas tree was twinkling with bright bulbs and Christmas ornaments Jason and her other children had made when they were small. There was the wonderful smell of cooking in the air and the fireplace was blazing.

Beth said. "You would think we were just like any other family, but tension was in the air." How can it be explained the feelings of parents sitting down for Christmas dinner with your son and his significant other?

"A gay homosexual person just walks into their lives like it is the normal part of a holiday." Phew! I realize many who are reading this book have no problem with the homosexual lifestyle. Therefore, you would find it difficult to understand why it would matter who comes to dinner. But this is Beth's story and beliefs.

The whole family had to readjust their thinking and be able to act like this was a Christmas like any other Christmas. The children opened presents, and they sang Christmas carols. There was tension, but Beth said she had to admire her two other children and their families. Everyone did their best to keep the day from being awkward.

The Homosexual Marriage Ceremony

Jason and Jonathon had been together for about a year when Tom and Beth received another phone call from Jason. He and Jonathon had decided to be married, and he would like them to come to the wedding. He also invited his brother and sister and his two boys, Chad and Justin.

The whole family was trying to decide what to do. This homosexual lifestyle and marriage was immoral to them. How does this work? Do you take this man to be your significant other for life until death do you part? Their Christian values and lifestyle clashed with Jason's new life.

Everyone felt it would be very awkward, but Beth made a decision for herself. She said, "I am going. I love Jason, and I do not want him to be saddened by the fact none of his family will be there." Soon, Tom and the others agreed to go.

Beth thought about this upcoming day and knew how difficult it would be on the whole family. She decided to call Jason and asked, "Could you please not kiss?" Jason agreed. They would just hug.

Again, Tom and Beth found they were in a place they could never fathom as part of their lives—in a church, watching their son marry another man. Jason looked very handsome in his tux, but what was wrong with this picture? Where was the bride in white?

Beth struggled with this change in her son. Life as she knew it did not feel normal. What is normal anyway? The *new normal* is a catchphrase these days, but she wanted to know, "How do we get back to normal?"

Struggles in life are inevitable. What burden might you be carrying today where you feel the cross is too heavy and the road too long? The gift of life is wonderful, but as we all know, it is inevitable that life comes with many struggles, heartaches, and hardship.

Each of us has a different road to follow, which God has laid out for us, and along this road will be some unexpected and unwanted surprises.

Your path is not, however, a surprise to God. He has known you from before you were born, and He knew what paths you would be taking. He knew the burdens you would have to carry. He also knew when your adult child decided to head down the wrong road. Thankfully, God did take the burden and help Beth to have the strength she needed.

Lightning Does Strike Twice

Beth is finally feeling she has a handle on this new change in all their lives and then…. the unthinkable happened! They say lightening never strikes twice in the same place. This was surely not the case in Beth's family. First, discovering their son was gay and then to get this next telephone call was beyond belief.

One Sunday morning, Tom and Beth received a phone call

from Jonathon. Quietly, he said, "I am sorry to have to tell you Jason died this morning." What? Why? Oh God, no! This can't be true! Jason was only thirty-seven years old. Jason had died? The very idea of Jason becoming homosexual and then dying an untimely death was inconceivable.

But it was true. Jason died of a heart attack that morning. Jonathon called 911, but it was too late. Jason was a large man and certainly could have lost some weight, but he never seemed to have any health problems.

In this one moment, the phone rings, and Tom and Beth went from having a wonderful amazing son to his being in a mortuary. Beth's disbelief was an understatement. Her heart was shattered again. Tom called the family, and with great sorrow, they all went to see Jason at the mortuary. No one could believe this terrible news.

They had hardly been able to think things through when there came another shock. Jonathon had Jason cremated the next day. They had no idea this was going to happen or if this is what Jason would have wanted.

Jonathon knew Jason for only a few years. This was their child of thirty-seven years. They were disappointed Jonathon never discussed this with them.

Beth ached with sadness. Her heart physically hurt and her spirit broken. She did not feel she really had a chance to say good-bye. She had many questions. Why did Jonathon have the cremation so quickly? Did Jason have pain? Did he know what was happening, or did he die easily in his sleep? Jonathon says he found Jason dead, so they really did not know.

There was an empty feeling within, and the pain was felt through the whole family. Jason's brother and sister, his two sons, friends, and even Cheryl, his ex-wife, grieved.

Beth prayed and asked God, "Will Jason go to heaven? Is he with you, God? Why did you take him so young? Why didn't you give Jason more time to change his lifestyle? Why?" Had anyone known Jason was not well? There is no way to stop all the questions that flood your mind.

They had a memorial service, and the church overflowed with family and friends mourning the death of such a good man. Jason was everything a parent could hope for. He was a wonderful son, a wonderful father, and a wonderful friend. He brought so much joy into their lives.

Jason had a colorful personality. He had amazing talent and showmanship, but there was this one thing, being homosexual. Being gay does not erase all the happy years with him. Now his light was extinguished, and what a bright light it was.

Tom and Beth were two grief-stricken parents at the memorial service not believing this new truth. He was gone. Jason was gone. They had prayed for Jason faithfully. They put their trust in God and knew God was in control of the future. Death was the last thing they would ever consider would happen. They were so busy trying to accept Jason for who he was.

Tom and Beth miss Jason enormously. He will never see the sunrise or the beautiful sunsets. He will never see his boys grow into men. They will never see him at the Thanksgiving dinner table again. What a void there will be in their lives without him.

The margin between life and death can be so small. Unexpected death is devastating. Jason had so much to offer the world and such talent to share with others. His time on earth was shortened, but in the time he was here, he was an inspiration to others.

How do we find peace after tragedy? The sadness and grief

of losing Jason was so deep and so devastating for Beth and her family. How do they ever reach joy again?

Even if you are a strong Christian, a tragedy like this will take so much out of you. Beth went through agonizing grief but was thankful she had God by her side as He always had been throughout her life. Their family found peace through faith in our Lord Jesus Christ.

What strength and courage it must have taken for Jason to tell his parents, his siblings, his wife, his children, and everyone he knew that he was homosexual. He had a choice to go on living the way he was living or to make a change. He decided it was a different life he wanted to live. He wanted to continue to serve God. Some Christians could not understand how he could continue serving God and be gay.

The Bible tells us of God's unmerited favor. His grace goes beyond our comprehension. Only God knows our soul, and He alone is the judge of how each of us live our lives.

I would not be so arrogant to think I could even begin to consider if Jason was in heaven. Have we not all sinned, even yesterday? There are so many things in life we do not understand. We can no more think through or explain being homosexual than it is to understand why small children are molested, or why so many people die of malnutrition in other countries.

How can we ever understand? We are not God, and it is not our place to judge. God alone knows the answers to these questions.

It was still unbelievable for Beth to think Jason had gone from being minister of music to being homosexual and then a much too early death.

After the funeral, weariness flooded over her. She could never remember being so tired. I could relate as I felt totally exhausted during our trials with Greg. Jesus tells us, "Come to me, all you who are weary and burdened, and I will give you rest." (Matt. 11:28)

I remember my heart was so heavy. A lot of sleep does not take away weary. A good meal does not take away weary. A vacation does not take away weary. There is a weariness of the soul.

When we are so weary and exhausted, we need to be fertilized just as wilting flowers need fertilizing. We need to be watered and cared for. Only Jesus can take away that weariness and that heavy burden.

Am I Being Too Cynical?

There is an interesting side note to this story. These are only my thoughts and not those of Jason's family. Jason and Jonathon had two friends, Dave and Shawn, who were a gay couple as well. Dave and Shawn had been living together for a long time and often socialized with Jason and Jonathon.

Dave as a good friend immediately came over to comfort Jonathon when he heard about Jason's death. Dave stayed a week to help Jonathon through the funeral arrangements and in any way he could. He decided to stay another week, then another week, then another week.

Finally, he left his partner, Shawn, and moved in with Jonathon. They are now a couple. It did not seem to me Jonathon grieved very long for Jason.

1. Jason was cremated the very next day.
2. Jason and Jonathon had close friends, another couple, Dave and Shawn. Dave moved in with Jonathon for a week to comfort him.

3. Dave stayed several weeks.
4. Dave broke off his relationship with Shawn.
5. Dave and Jonathon are now a couple.
6. We have been told Jonathon's previous partner also died unexpectedly.

I guess it was just a remarkable coincidence. My husband says I have always had an overzealous and suspicious mind. He is right, and my suspicious mind is probably working overtime.

Beth had difficult questions on her mind regarding Jason. Where was he? Where would he spend eternity? Is he in hell? You may have painful concerns about your own adult child. Where will they spend eternity?

I would like to share some of my feelings about this in the next chapter. I do not have answers, but I have food for thought. We all have different opinions on the hereafter. I hope you will gain some insight from reading chapter 10.

Questions to Ponder

1. Are you spiritually ready for unexpected and unwanted surprises in life?

2. Do you suffer rejection from your son or daughter? Do you need to forgive your adult child?

Those who trust in the Lord
are like Mount Zion,
which cannot be shaken,
but endures forever.
(Ps. 125.1)

Chapter 10

Eternity Matters

I f eternity matters, it sheds a different light on everything that happens in our life.

Whether you are a Christian or not, every person has to wonder, "Is this all?" Is our life here on earth over if we die young like Jason, or we die at eighty years old as my parents? I certainly do not know the answer to all the "big questions."

Beth had some questions, and they were painful questions. She was hurting and wanted to know where her son was now. She asked, "What happened to Jason's soul?" Beth wanted to find something in the Bible to help her understand if Jason was in heaven. Will she see him again?

Beth grew up as a Christian and followed the teachings of the Bible the best she could. She accepted Christ as her Savior at an early age. She trusted God in all things, asking for His guidance. She taught her children to know and love God.

After the shock of finding out Jason was homosexual, she put on the armor of God to fight Satan. She prayed continually, but Jason's decisions in life were not going to change.

Beth had always felt a guardian angel would look out for her family and not let any harm come to her children. She said to me, "Aren't we to run to God for refuge and strength when we face trials? I have always known God is my fortress. This is what I did."

The Certainty of Eternity

She questioned, "The Bible says anyone whose name is not in the book of life will be thrown into the lake of fire. Has my child been thrown into the lake of fire? Was Jason born gay? Did he become this way in his adolescence years? Did I choose to be heterosexual when I was young, or was I just born this way?"

Beth believed in healing and prayed for Jason's healing as did many friends and family. She knew God could heal Jason, and He could take these homosexual desires away. Why didn't God heal him? Why would Jason go to hell, if we prayed for his healing, and God chose not to heal him?

I understand how Beth felt. The Bible says, "All things work together for good to those who love God." I had a problem with this scripture. Why was my son born bipolar? Why did my son go to a federal prison at nineteen years old? It took me a long time of studying the Bible and prayer before I was able to accept the circumstances of our family's tragedy with Greg.

I would like to share what God taught me through my studies and His speaking to my heart. Maybe you have fears of what has happened or will happen to your wayward child. God has given me an assurance of my son spending eternity with Him.

I seriously thought about Beth's questions concerning her son. Jason accepted Christ as his Savior when he was young. There was no question he loved God and, in his adult life, continued to serve God. Just as a clarification of my beliefs, I do not believe, "Once saved, always saved."

Jason told Beth he prayed for years, "God, forgive me for my thoughts. I don't want to have these thoughts and desires. Please, God, don't stop loving me." When Jason made the decision to give into the homosexual lifestyle, he did not think he was going to burn in hell for eternity.

Jason's Struggle

The reason for the struggle Jason went through all those years is because *he did love God and had accepted Jesus as his Savior.* If he didn't have a heart for God, there would be no struggle. He would not care what God thought. He would not care what anyone thought. He was going to live his life as he pleased, but that was not the case. His battle never stopped.

We are born into a sinful world with an inherited sinful nature, and we all battle sin throughout our journey. The Bible tells us we will have trials here on earth, and through those trials, we will grow spiritually.

The struggle *is* the process of our journey and our walk with the Lord. There is value in the struggle. We do not thank God for our trials, but we do thank Him for the inner strength and character He is building in us.

There are many Christians who struggle with sexual immorality, which includes adultery, premarital sex, pornography, homosexual behavior, lust, and more.

Other Christians have struggles with different sin in their lives. Some struggle with lying, cheating, bitterness, gossip, stealing, drunkenness, hatred, envy, and more. We all make mistakes. We sin.

Paul had something very unique to say about sin. In fact, I find a little humor in these next verses.

> I know that nothing good lives in me, that is,
> in my sinful nature. For I have the desire to do
> what is good, but I cannot carry it out. For what
> I do is not the good I want to do—no, the evil I

do not want to do—this I keep on doing. Now if I do what I do not want to do, it is no longer I who do it, but it is sin living in me that does it. (Rom. 7:18–20)

And Paul goes on about this dilemma.…

"What a wretched man I am! Who will rescue me from this body of death? Thanks be to God – through Jesus Christ our Lord." (Rom. 7:24–25)

Isn't that how we all are? Isn't that how Jason was? Paul explained it better than I ever could. We want to do good, but we do wrong! We do not want to sin, but we do! We consciously work at not sinning and then we sin.

Thankfully, God looks at the heart, and He knows who wants to follow Him and who does not. We all struggle with sin, and none of us deserve to be saved and have eternity with Christ. Our Father in heaven looks at our hearts. He knew Jason's heart.

I have a friend who has loved the Lord for many years. He is also an alcoholic. Self-determination did not help him to stop drinking. When we become a Christian, this desire to sin still follows us and we cannot fight sin with our own strength.

God sends us the Holy Spirit to become part of us to give us power over sin. And when we fail, God lovingly reaches down for us. The difference is we are in a lifelong process of learning to be more like Jesus. Our struggle in life's journey *is* with sin.

Who decided being homosexual is a worse sin than other sins? Is Jason's sin maybe just a more glaring sin than yours or mine? For some reason, it seems the church and many Christians believe this sin is greater than other sins mentioned in the Bible. Does God look at sexual immorality as worse than stealing or gossiping?

The Bible clearly says homosexuals will not inherit the kingdom of God. It also says drunkards, the greedy, swindlers, nor will thieves inherit the kingdom of God. This is probably the verse that most people are familiar with.

> Do you not know that the wicked will not inherit the Kingdom of God? Do not be deceived: Neither the sexual immoral nor idolaters nor adulterers nor male prostitutes nor homosexual offenders nor thieves nor the greedy nor drunkards nor slanders nor swindlers will inherit the kingdom of God.
>
> And that is what some of you were. But you were washed, you were sanctified, you were justified in the name of the Lord Jesus Christ and by the Holy Spirit of our God. (1 Cor. 6:9–11)

This verse is very clear. Will all drunkards and slanderers and those who gossip also go to hell? Will those who cheat on their taxes, take the Lord's name in vain, take advantage of others, or are full of anger lose their salvation?

But wait! … What about these verses?

> Therefore, there is no condemnation for those who are in Christ Jesus, because through Jesus

Christ the law of the Spirit of life set me free from the law of sin and death. (Rom. 8:1)

All have sinned and come short of the glory of God and are justified freely by His grace through redemption that came by Christ Jesus. (Rom. 3:23–24)

Old Testament

Following the laws of the Old Testament, we are all powerless to be saved. We are unable to keep all the laws because of our sinful nature.

Therefore, we cannot be saved by obeying the laws. All we would get is frustration and discouragement because try as we might, we fail. This can make us feel hopeless, but praise God, when we get to the New Testament, God gives us His plan of salvation.

The Bible also clearly says, "The wages of sin is death, but the gift of God is eternal life through Jesus Christ our Lord." (Rom. 6:23)

We are all sinners until Christ died on the cross in our place. We were lost and dead in our sins. Praise God the blood of Jesus freed us from the snares of sin. We would surely all have death, if the wages of sin are death, but for the grace of God.

We all have sinned, each and every one of us. Did we sin today in our hearts? Did we sin yesterday? Because of Jesus dying on the cross for our sins, we no longer have to carry the guilt of failing to do right. Of course, we are to follow God's ways and commandments, but as we trust in God, we are loved and forgiven.

Justification

What an amazing word. What does justification mean? Justification is God declaring us "not guilty" for our sins. "If you confess with your mouth Jesus is Lord and believe in your heart that God raised him from the dead, you are justified in Christ." (Rom. 10:9) We have been justified through Jesus Christ dying on the cross for our sins!

A church member came to her pastor and asked, "If I can't overcome a particular sin, have I lost my salvation?" What if a person has accepted Christ but cannot overcome a sin they are struggling with? Are they lost eternally?

Some Christians believe God would forgive someone who confesses their sins, but if they died with unconfessed sins, they would be lost forever. What about our own hidden faults or our unintentional sins? Are we forgiven?

We are saved by *grace, which is unearned and undeserved favor from God.* Through our faith in Jesus Christ, we stand before God justified "not guilty." Our record is wiped clean as though we never sinned.

If you go to court and the judge says you are not guilty, this means all charges are removed. You have nothing showing on the court records.

When our sins are forgiven, we are declared not guilty, and we have a clean record. However, true confession of our sins also involves a commitment not to continue to sin. 1 Jn. 1:8 tells us "If we claim to be without sin, we deceive ourselves." Praise God for justification.

The question of our eternal life has more to do with our relationship with Jesus. God looks at the recesses of a person's heart. Of course, we want to flee from sinful things and pursue God. His desire is that our salvation will result in our turning from sin. What is in our heart? Are we struggling, trying, working at, and praying for God's help?

Many churches and many Christians are quick to put judgment on the gay and lesbian lifestyle. Did we decide somewhere along the way that some sins are no longer considered "too awfully bad," and others sins such as homosexual behavior deserves death and hell? It seems to me the churches "focus" on many things have changed.

For instance:

> Matthew tells us if you look at a woman in lust, you have already committed adultery. Will that person be facing hell?
>
> Divorce was looked down on in certain denominations until this generation. If you were divorced, you could not hold a position as elder, or even teach a class in church.
>
> If divorced, you could not remarry except under certain conditions. Today divorce is accepted in most denominations.
>
> Adultery with your neighbor's wife will be punished by death. Today, our laws would certainly not put someone to death.
>
> Unfortunately, premarital sex has become the norm in many areas of our world.

Of course, it goes without saying that because churches and social media have become more tolerant does not mean these sins are accepted by God. They are not!

Who are we to make moral judgments on anyone for we

all have sinned! We are all struggling on our journey to overcome sin and to become more like Christ daily. Are we not?

We are trying to become more like Christ, which means we are not like Christ now, but we are stretching toward being more like Him. Therefore, during that time of stretching, we will sin, and we will fail, but what is in your heart?

I saw Jason's battle with being homosexual and I had to ask myself, Where does Jason stand with God? Do homosexuals have a right to consider that God still loves them? Are gay and lesbians deserving of God's love? We who have sinned as well, we seem to accept that God still loves us.

This is what I know for sure. God is a loving God who loved Jason more than his own mother loved him. God shows us throughout the Bible of His mercy and grace? God knew our human nature would pull us toward sin which is why He sent His son to die on the cross to take our place.

There is another wonderful verse that I relate to Jason. "Being confident of this, He who began a good work in you will carry it on to completion until the day of Christ Jesus." (Phil. 1:6) There was never a doubt that God started a good work in Jason.

I would not want anyone coming to the conclusion that I am okay with the homosexual lifestyle. I am absolutely against it based on the Bible. What I am saying is I accept the gift of salvation not only for myself but for my children and others. I cannot judge.

The Sun *Will* come up in the Morning!

Whether you believe in eternity or not, the sun will come up in the morning, and the stars will come out at night. The sun stays a safe distance away from the earth. If the sun comes too close to the earth, the earth would be scorched and destroyed. If the sun wanders too far away, our earth would freeze. It continues to stay exactly where God has control over it.

Whether you believe in eternity or not, we continue to breathe in and out each day. Our bodies continue to circulate blood to the heart, and the kidneys flush out our systems. Our bodies continue to fight off disease.

Whether you believe in eternity or not, there is a date you will die, and it is not up to you when that date is. Each one of our lives has an expiration date.

Whether you believe in eternity or not, the beauty of God's creation continues to amaze us each and every day. The cherry tree loses its blooms in the winter and will bloom again in the spring. The rainbow is still an awesome thing to see.

If eternity does not matter, then what is the point of life? I find it easy to believe God created the heavens and the earth. It is much easier for me to believe in an Almighty Creator than to believe there was a big explosion, and here we are.

To believe in the Big Bang Theory is to believe you could put a bomb under an airplane, blow it into the air into millions of pieces, and it comes back down to the ground in the form of an airplane again. Not only in the form of an airplane, but this airplane's engine will start up, and you can take off and fly!

Really? It is much easier for me to believe in God. Therefore, if I believe in God; I believe in eternity.

I cannot imagine life here on earth is *all there is*. I believe both in God and in the eternal glory God promises. Because of this belief, I have no fear of what happens to me and my children through our temporary life here on earth. Yes, there is pain and suffering through the process of life, but there is no fear.

If I thought there was even a remote chance that a child of mine would go to hell, I would never have had children. My husband said to take this sentence out of the book as it might be misunderstood. What I am trying to express with this statement is my total faith in God tells me to trust God with my children. I trust Him completely.

Our struggles here on earth are momentary troubles of which we are going through knowing we have eternal glory ahead of us. Our life span here is like a fleeting moment compared to eternity. When a person accepts Jesus Christ as their Savior, they can cope much better with struggles because of *"the certainty of eternity."*

There is so much in this world I don't understand, but because of my personal relationship with Jesus, I am able to trust God even when I do not understand.

If I don't understand a verse in the Bible, it doesn't throw me into doubt. I believe the Bible is God's Word. We do not understand everything in the Bible. Nevertheless, I *choose* to believe.

We do not understand why we have affliction here on earth, some more than others. We do not understand why the moon comes out each night. I do not understand why my son has had to struggle so in life. I do not understand why the holocaust happened.

We are not God, and His ways are not our ways. "As the heavens are higher than the earth so are my ways and my thoughts than your thoughts." (Isa. 55:9)

Is Jason in heaven with our Savior? Only our Heavenly Father knows this. He was continuing in his homosexual lifestyle, but was he struggling with it? He never stopped loving the Lord. Was he saying the night before he went to sleep, "Oh,

God, I know this is wrong. Forgive me!" Did God decide to take him home right then to heaven?

I'm glad I am not God! He is in control of the universe. I'm glad He is making all the *big decisions*. All we have to do is, "Have the faith of a mustard seed."

And now…. onto our next story.

I hope you will find encouragement from our next story. This is the story of a Christian mother who faced the tragedy of drug abuse with her son. This was a young man who tried to kill his mother and almost succeeded. These tragedies are things we read about in the newspaper never thinking they would happen to us.

Questions to Ponder

1. How much serious thought have you given to eternity? Can you write an entire page on your belief or non-belief in eternity?

2. Do you feel all sins are equal in God's eyes? Do you believe this following verse to be true?

The wages of sin are death,
but the gift of God
is eternal life through
Jesus Christ our Lord.
(Rom. 6:23)

Part Three

Stranger in the House

Chapter 11

My Son's Downward Spiral

David always called me Mom, but this time, he said, "*Mother*," in a very matter-of-fact voice, "I'm going to kill you." I turned around. "David what are you saying?" But you know, instantly, I knew he meant it. There was no question in my mind he meant what he said. He was going to kill me.

I appreciate Barbara allowing me to share her story with you. I pray it gives you encouragement in dealing with your own adult child.

As parents, we go through many emotions watching our children making bad choices. This story is about Barbara's son, David, who almost succeeded in killing her. It was an unbelievably difficult time in Barbara's life, and she was finding it hard to understand what was happening to her and her family.

Barbara was married at seventeen and had three children in the next five years, two boys and a girl. She was happy being a mother and wife. She wanted to be the best mom and wife she could be. She and her kids were involved in many activities.

They attended a Bible teaching church. She was a Sunday school teacher and sang in the church choir. Her children were happily involved in activities at both church and school. Their father did not go to church except on rare occasions.

David was Barbara's second son. I know it is hard to imagine, but Barbara says it seemed from the time he was born; her husband just did not like David. Even as a baby, you could feel it. Others in the family noticed it as well. David's grandparents gave him extra attention as they wanted to make him feel special to help release the stress when his dad was around.

David had a skin problem when he was first born. It hurt Barbara when she heard his father telling someone negative things about their new baby's skin. He was beautiful to her. Their first son, Paul, was the apple of his dad's eye, while David was ignored by his father.

David seemed to be the one who was always in trouble. All three of their children could be involved in misbehaving, but David was always blamed by his dad and had to be punished. His dad was an intelligent man, but he could put you down by words and actions in such a belittling way. The way David's father treated him was emotionally crippling.

David also had a stuttering problem, which started when he was four years old. This made him very self-conscious. Thankfully, it did improve over time. He was a very bright intelligent boy, quite sensitive, and would never intentionally hurt anyone. He excelled in sports and music and was always looking for and needing his dad's acceptance.

His dad would tell David he was proud of him, but Barbara knew and so did David he was not always sincere. David felt his dad was never happy with anything he did. Barbara tried to be his cheerleader and to show him how proud she was of him.

They started having problems with David when he was in the tenth grade. He began skipping school and not following through on what he was asked to do. Barbara didn't know it at the time, but he started taking drugs at the age of sixteen.

Barbara told me she was so naïve about drug abuse that it never occurred to her that David's behavior was caused by drugs. It took her a long time to fully accept this fact. A few years later, he told her that within a week of starting drugs, he was using LSD.

Barbara's first inclination of something more serious being wrong with David was seeing the crowd he began to hang out with. One day, she came home from work for lunch, which she rarely did and found all these young men in their home, none of whom she knew. There was loud music blaring, and they were all drinking. These were none of David's usual friends. She told them to get out immediately and not return. David was high at that time, and it scared her.

Another time, David was talking with similar people out in the street in front of their home. They all looked older. *Who are these people?* They were not the kind of individuals you would want for your child to be associated with. These new friends obviously had a big influence on him.

It was during this time Barbara realized how much David was drinking as she could smell alcohol when he came home. She was worried and felt ill equipped to handle these problems. It also made for an unstable environment for her other children.

Before all this happened, Barbara talked with her children and told them, "If I ever thought you kids were getting into drugs or stealing, I would turn you in to the police." They were shocked. "Mom, you wouldn't do that?" She told them, "Yes, I would because I would want it to stop immediately. I would not want it to continue."

Barbara said those words, but when all these things were actually happening with David, that is not what she did. She knew David was taking drugs, but she felt she could talk to him and help him through this rebellious stage.

David would deny ever taking drugs, and everyone wanted

to believe him. He told her once he could con anyone into believing whatever he wanted. That is exactly what he was doing to her. She tried different kinds of discipline with him, but he continued to rebel. Finally, one day, she found empty drug capsules in his room. David always had excuses for what he was doing, but this was hard to explain his way out of.

This was the typical story you might hear about in the news of any teenager getting on drugs. Drug addiction totally changed David. He had been a very good student. David was a student body officer and played goalie on the water polo team. He was first chair trombone in the band and drum major of his high school. He had high goals and was working toward being an eagle scout. David was a son you could be proud of. Probably just like your child.

Drugs Were Destroying David

David told Barbara the reason he started using drugs was not just to party, but he wanted to find himself. He really wanted to get into himself and find out what made him tick. His behavior became more erratic. He always explained the reasons for his bad behavior and felt everyone should understand and accept his explanations.

David's father was often gone from home on business. During the time Barbara was having these problems with David, his father was working in Saudi Arabia. It was during this same time she discovered her marriage of almost twenty years was crumbling.

She was devastated when she learned her husband and her oldest friend were having an affair. This was not just a short-term affair, but she learned they had been seeing each other for years! She was crushed and brokenhearted.

She knew he had affairs in the past. Phone calls would come in, and when she would answer, they would hang up. One time, he told her he was coming home for a few days from Saudi Arabia. Later, she found he had been in San Diego for some time before coming home. With her marriage in trouble, she was concerned for her children and their future. This was really the end of their marriage as her husband wanted to be free.

She was already dealing with so much drama with David and was feeling emotionally drained. From the time of discovering her husband's affair, it was two weeks later when David was arrested for having drugs in his car. Barbara had to go through all the challenges of David's arrest and drug use alone. Attorneys and court dates were things she was totally unfamiliar with.

At the same time, David's cousin who was only sixteen years old was killed in an automobile accident. David was very close to his cousin, and he was devastated. This was a shock to their whole family, and it was another thing which added to David's decline.

Barbara could not believe all of this was coming down on her and her family. So much, so fast! She always felt she had a blessed life, never having any trauma or upheaval in their home. Now it seemed with David, there was always a new problem to deal with.

David had developed a disregard for authority whether it was at school, the police, or his parents. He became very secretive and was not going to school regularly. Eventually, Barbara could not believe anything David said and began to realize how little she could do to help him.

She kept up a facade and carried on with her job. At times,

she would go to work, and her head would be pounding. The darkness of David's drug and alcohol use was like a dark cloud over her head following her each day.

Barbara was a librarian, and one day, as she was leaving the library, she told me she really felt she was going to crack up, and someone may just find her on the ground. It was like an explosion in her head. She wondered if she was going to have a nervous breakdown. She was exhausted and glad to make it home.

Barbara prayed for David to be able to get off drugs. It was still inconceivable to her that her David would have a drug addiction. Being a positive person, she continued to believe they were going to make it through this difficult time.

She had heard testimonies of other young people on drugs finding Christ, and God delivered them from their drug use. She was reaching out for hope for David.

Barbara's parents were wonderful Christians and were also praying for David. Other family and friends were praying. One night, when David came home, it was obvious he was on drugs. Barbara yelled at him, "Just stop!" All he had to do was stop the drugs, get serious about work or school. In her frustration, she really thought it would be that easy, and he could "just stop."

Of course, this is not the case. Addiction is a serious illness, and it will completely dominate your life. You become obsessed, controlled, and overpowered by addiction to drugs. You don't just stop, and you are back on track. This was a world that had never really existed in Barbara's mind. Never would a child of hers be involved with substance abuse.

David grew up an intelligent and capable teenager; however, the life he was leading now was reckless and dangerous. Barbara tried to talk with him about the importance of education. She was trying to show him how his friends were moving on with their lives, but David had no interest in college or getting a job.

She couldn't reach him with the truth of what was happening with the drugs. He refused to listen to any advice. She tried a different approach, explaining how the drugs would affect his body and how he was destroying his body and mind but there is no reasoning with someone on drugs.

David had become so defensive; it was difficult to carry on a conversation with him. His anger would flare up. At times, he became withdrawn. He was very indifferent to anything Barbara had to say. It seemed he was incapable of thinking clearly about anything. He had this rapid talking and sometimes he trembled.

Barbara had used all her arguments and persuasive power to convince him to change his life. She began to realize her David was no longer the sweet child she raised. His actions were surreal. He did not care what his mom or anyone thought because he was in an altered state of mind most of the time.

She was feeling desperate each day, worrying about him. She was worried how David would be the next time she saw him. Will he be stumbling because of alcohol? Will he be hyper on drugs? This burden sapped every ounce of energy she had. She had been praying continually for him.

One day in particular, she was home alone and felt she needed to talk to God. She went into her bedroom, fell on her knees, and cried out to God to take this burden from her.

She prayed, "Lord, I cannot go any further. I know you love David, and I know you have not abandoned us, but I am so discouraged." God reminded her again she was not alone. He was right there with her each and every day.

Our lives can be difficult at times and full of despair, but at the same time, we are learning to depend on God. Through this process, we mature as Christians. Barbara had prayed many times before, but this was different. She felt lighter when she stood up. It was like a huge weight lifted. Needless to say, her problems were still there, but she knew she had Jesus by her side.

Barbara was dealing with so many other issues aside from David. Her marriage was in trouble.

In devotions she read, "Call upon me in the day of trouble. I will deliver you and you will honor me." (Ps. 50:15) This was certainly her day of trouble. Today, this was a scripture just for her.

She was trying to stay strong and have faith. God wants us to take that first step of faith, and He will show us the next step and the next and the next. This sounds so easy, doesn't it? We all know, however, it is very difficult to *let go* of problems and let God take over. Even though He is the Creator of the universe, we still foolishly think we can handle our problems ourselves!

There are times we make things hard for ourselves and we become our own worst enemy. We say we trust God and find ourselves taking the burden back the next day. We want God to answer in a different way, but God's way is always the best way. He has a better plan for us and our loved one than we could ever imagine.

Out of Control

David was on a downward spiral and out of control. While Barbara was going through this hurt and pain, a real blessing came her way. She met Bob, her present husband. She was trusting God the best she could while going through divorce and the handling of David. God knew she needed a friend by her side. She needed someone to walk with her through this time of her life, and God sent Bob her way.

They met at a support group she had heard about, which was to find help for your teenager. Bob had such a wonderful personality. He was sweet, and his love for Jesus was so strong. Barbara just melted.

It was God's perfect timing! Within eight months, they were married. I believe God brought Bob into her life at the perfect time to help her over the many hurdles and obstacles she was going to be facing. He was a wonderful influence on her kids. They loved him and still do.

Bob helped David in many ways. He helped him to get a job and to buy a truck. They encouraged David to get his GED. David was very smart but was no longer able to follow through on anything. Being on drugs is a terrible life as this addiction consumes your life totally. A person's personality completely changes, and David was not the same person.

Barbara never blamed God. She probably asked why, but she never had the feeling some people do in becoming angry at God. She felt her life had been so blessed that it was just her turn. She continued to be confident they would be successful in helping David get his life turned around.

Ever since Bob and she were married, they prayed together each morning. They would pray for their day and ask God to help them through the day. I believe those prayers put a shield around Barbara to help her through the unbelievable and terrifying drama she was about to face.

David was nineteen years old and having a hard time holding down a job. When he would lose a job, it was always someone else's fault. He would say he was going to work, but of course, he didn't. David's bizarre behavior had escalated beyond what she and Bob could deal with.

David had been living with his older brother in his spare bedroom, and Barbara knew things were not going well. One day, she decided to stop by to see David without calling ahead. Her older son said, "Mom, this is not a good time." She knew something was wrong. She insisted on seeing David.

When she opened the door to his room, she was totally paralyzed with shock. It is one thing to know your son is on drugs and occasionally see him in a highly agitated state, but this was an entirely different scene for her.

She was in no way prepared for what she saw. David was sitting on the floor incoherent. He looked as if he hadn't bathed in weeks. It was a sight that is hard to ever get out of your mind. This gave Barbara instantly the complete picture of how the drug abuse was destroying David.

Addiction to drugs is like having a parasite. Years ago, I had traveled to a third world country and picked up some foreign bug. When I came home, I was sick. This was not being a little sick. I was sick for over a year.

My doctor tried one antibiotic after another. Nothing worked. I tried one doctor after another. I even went to an Indian doctor as that was the country I had spent time in. I guess I thought he may recognize the parasite I had. Of course, he was probably born in America and went to an American medical school.

He explained something to me about parasites that made sense. If you start with one parasite in your body, it turns into two. Those two parasites turn into four, those four turn into eight, and those eight turn into sixteen. And on and on. Before you know it, you have hundreds of these parasites, and it takes a very long time to rid your body of all of them.

You take an antibiotic, and it kills almost all of them. Some of those parasites, maybe just one or two, hide behind some part of your body like a muscle. Then ....those two hiding parasites become four. Four become eight, and before you know it, you have hundreds again. No antibiotic helped.

It took over a year before my body completely was rid of whatever parasite I had. There is no question in my mind God healed me. The parasite I was battling was not susceptible to any antibiotic I tried.

Addiction to drugs is very much the same. Once drugs enter your body, the desire for them takes over. This is not something you take an antibiotic for, and it goes away. Your body begins to require the drug, and the desire becomes overpowering.

David had become dysfunctional. While staying at his brother's house, he was staying heavily drugged. Barbara was stunned to find out he had tried several times to overdose. He said he wanted to die. She really did not believe him and felt it was the drugs talking. She could not understand how anyone would really want to die.

There are times drug and alcohol addiction may be stopped through therapy and the different programs offered around the country, but it is very difficult. Anyone who is addicted to drugs can fight it with everything within them, but often the drugs win out.

If your adult child is fighting drugs or alcohol, there is a point you realize it is out of your control. God has been waiting for you to call on Him.

Questions to Ponder

1. Do you feel your child is out of control? Can you elaborate on what has happened to them?

2. Do you feel you have done all you can? You may need to think back years, but make a list of all the things you have done to help them.

Let Him who walks in the dark,
Who has no light
Trust in the name of the Lord.
And rely on his God.
(Isa. 50:10b)

Chapter 12

Help! It's A Tsunami!

Barbara was watching her son go downhill. David was in an undercurrent. The strongest swimmer can be caught in an undercurrent and not be able to free himself. He may be an excellent swimmer, but he still may drown. This is what was happening to David. He was caught in an undercurrent of addiction. He tried the best he could to free himself, but could not. Bob, Barbara, and their whole family were praying for him.

We try to raise our children with good morals and values, don't we? Barbara knew in her heart her children were going to turn out as well adjusted and confident young adults. We teach them the difference between right and wrong. We teach them why we do not want them drinking, smoking, and taking drugs.

We believe they will follow those rules. No parent expects their children would turn to drugs. Something like this happens in dysfunctional families.

Barbara believed her children would be safe from all the terrible headlines you read of other unfortunate children. She did not see this coming as she assumed and took for granted her children would never drink alcohol or take drugs.

Barbara was facing many challenges at one time. When the storms of life come, you will be tossed to and fro. You stand up and the next wave knocks you down again. She was having trouble sleeping and concentrating. She prayed, "God, I think this is more than a storm. I think it's more than a hurricane or a tornado. I think it's a Tsunami!"

The Tsunami is the grand-daddy of all storms. Some people have compared it to a tidal wave, but it is far worse. It does not resemble a normal sea wave or a breaking wave on the shore. It is a rising wave with an unbelievable magnitude of force. It can reach over one hundred feet tall and move at five hundred miles an hour.

Help Me God! I Think It's A Tsunami!

Barbara was feeling the storms of life were going to be much more devastating than she could imagine. She was saying to God, "This is not just your normal storm. Help me, God."

Usually when there is a storm brewing, the clouds begin looking dark, the wind will blow, and you might hear thunder and lightning. You have a bit of a warning. There are times, however, when the storm will take you by surprise as a tsunami will.

Growing up in Ohio, I became familiar at a young age of fierce storms. When I was about eight years old, a tornado hit our small town. It had been raining, and the trees bent over from the winds. I remember the tornado hit, and it sounded like a train roaring through our house.

Our family as everyone else in our small town took shelter from the storm. We had a cellar we ran to. My siblings and I were scared! We were young and had not seen anything like this before. After the tornado blew past, we came out and saw the most unbelievable sight. The damage the tornado left was devastating.

Our church which was near our home was totally demolished as were many stores and houses. The roof and the first floor of the church were all now in the basement. Many church members and friends met us at the church and were shocked and overwhelmed at how much damage the tornado had caused.

I remember my mother crying, and many people gathering together for comfort. Eventually, everyone settled down. Even though I was a child, I remember my dad and others saying, "All right, let's get started rebuilding."

Barbara was going through an emotional storm; the damage was also devastating. She was definitely finding herself in a grave situation. She was battling the storm daily.

God, what do we do? First we take shelter from the storm as we did when the tornado came. Take shelter in God who is our refuge.

And then we too, have the emotional damage from the storm to deal with. We can feel bitterness, anxiety, and overwhelming trauma. Just as with the aftermath of the tornado, we have to find the strength to say, "All right, let's get started rebuilding."

I have had many prayers answered in my life as I am sure Barbara had. So when the biggest challenge of all comes, is trusting God any different? We must remember our largest challenges and our largest problems in life are nothing compared to how great our God is. He is our shelter in times of life's storms. He is our refuge. He is our fortress.

David's life was out of control. He had been living with his older brother Paul for some time. Paul traveled on his job and was getting ready to move to a new job in another city. He was worried about what was going to happen to David because he would not have a place to live. Paul's moving away threw David into more of a tailspin.

David had stayed with Bob and Barbara for short times but

they would not allow him to lie around doing nothing. He knew he had to be productive in some way, or he could not stay at their home. They tried tough love with David to make him understand he had to stand on his own.

When Paul moved, David had to move, and Barbara did not know where he was. They were worried as they had not heard from him in three weeks. Barbara called some of his friends, but they were not able to find him. Later, she learned he was staying with friends who were also on drugs.

I do not think anyone can realize how discouraging it is to have a son or daughter on drugs unless they have been through it. Barbara was about to face a much more serious problem then drugs. When tragedy comes into our lives, we need God more than ever. Satan tries to destroy the mind of a parent. With such pain and sorrow, we desperately need God.

Satan works overtime at night. Have you noticed that? At night, our minds will race with all the terrible things that might happen, and worry can consume us. There were times when I was going through my crisis with Greg that I had to sit up in bed and say to Satan, "Stop. In the name of Jesus, stop!"

I ask God to give me sleep, give me rest, and stop my mind from racing and thinking the worst. Barbara needed her mind to stop racing as well.

Just as a body armor will protect the warrior from his enemy. The armor of the Lord protects us when Satan uses his power against us. Satan has the power of evil and darkness, but all we have to do is put on the armor of God and take our stand.

> Finally be strong in the Lord and in His mighty
> power. Put on the full armor of God so that you
> can take your stand against the devil's schemes.

For our struggle is not against flesh and blood,
but against the rulers, against the authorities,
against the powers of this dark world and against
the spiritual forces of evil in the heavenly realms.
(Eph. 6:11)

Am I Going to Die?

One day, Barbara was home sick with the flu. She was standing at the kitchen window. She looked up and saw David going down the hill in front of their house on a bicycle. When she saw him, he turned and looked back at her. He knew she had seen him, so he turned around and came back to the house. Barbara went to the door, relieved to finally see him and know that he was okay.

He came into the house acting very strange. He was bouncing around and acting odd. She knew he must be on some kind of drug. He left, but he told her later he had come that day to get one of Bob's guns. She still doesn't know why or what he was planning to do with it.

The next morning, Barbara was still not feeling well. The doorbell rang, and it was David. She explained it to me like this, "His eyes looked glassy. His skin tone was strange and peculiar. He looked gray and disheveled. He needed a shave. He had these wrinkled old clothes on."

He said he came for his backpack. He wanted her to unlock the garage and help him look for it. Barbara told him it was not there as he had taken it some time ago, but he said he didn't have it, and he still wanted to look for it. They went into the garage, and he was acting strange. David was her son, and she certainly did not have a fear of him, but she was feeling uncomfortable.

Back in the house, Barbara went into the kitchen, and David

went into the bathroom. He was there for what seemed like a long time. Later, she learned he was taking more drugs. Barbara was at the sink cleaning up the dishes, and she heard him come out of the bathroom. He was about ten or twelve feet away from her. This is what she told me happened.

"David always called me Mom. This time, he said, 'Mother,' in a very matter of fact voice, 'I'm going to kill you.' I turned around. 'David, what are you saying?' But you know, instantly, I knew he meant it. There was no question in my mind he meant what he said. He was going to kill me. I could see it in his eyes."

Can you imagine the kind of shock Barbara would have felt? There was no time to think rationally. He said in a cocky strange voice, "What's the matter? Are you afraid?" There was a terrifying look in his eyes.

Barbara's kitchen window was open. Later, she replayed this scenario over and over in her mind. What should she have done? She flipped the window open more and started screaming. There happened to be a delivery man across the street unloading something into their neighbor's garage. He had the motor running in his truck and did not hear her.

She told me, "The next thing I know I was on the floor. David's knee was on my neck. There was a desperate struggle. He had his hand over my face, and I was suffocating. I truly felt this was it. I was trying to scream, and he was saying, 'Shut up, shut up, shut up' as he was coming down on me. I felt sure I was going to die. We struggled. I was able to barely move my head to the side, and I said out loud, Jesus, forgive him."

She continued, "I had no thought of praying. I just said, 'Jesus, forgive him.' When I said this, his hands instantly released me. He got off me and said, 'You and your Jesus.'"

Barbara was thankful the word *Jesus* came to her because there is power in the name of Jesus. This caused him to release her, but this was just the beginning of a frightening day of fear.

A Faithful Prayer Life

Barbara knew Jesus in a personal way. She did not need to cry out with a long prayer, asking God to spare her life and help her. She just said the name Jesus. David was still on drugs, but with hearing the name of Jesus, he let go of his mother.

You see, Barbara was not alone. The Holy Spirit dwells within us and is able to help sustain us in every situation that comes our way. God has all power over Satan. God sends his guardian angel to guard his children in time of danger. Barbara is a child of the King, and she was in danger. She did not need to stop and pray while this was happening because God was already there.

Bob and Barbara were healthy spiritually. They were praying and asking for God's guidance daily. When you have a relationship with Jesus and a tragedy comes, you are spiritually ready. You already have the armor of God on. The enemy may take you by surprise, but you are prepared. That is not to say Barbara was not afraid and felt fear.

Have you ever been to Carlsbad Caverns? While visiting, a guide will take you farther and farther down into the cave. While touring the caverns, they will turn out the lights to show you what real darkness is. It is so dark you cannot see your hand in front of you. It is just the most terrible and frightening feeling. Of course, you know they are going to turn the lights on again shortly.

Imagine trying to find your way out of the caverns in the complete darkness. It would be frightening and could be impossible. You may not find your way out.

When darkness comes into our lives as it did with Barbara

that day, how do we find our way out of the darkness? The difference is God finds us. We do not find our way on our own. He finds us. He is always near.

When we need God's help, the Bible tells us we can cry out to Him. He is there, that minute, that second. This is what Barbara did. She had a faithful prayer life, and all she had to do was say the name Jesus.

Questions to Ponder

1. Have you ever been afraid of your own child?

2. Do you fear what is going to happen to your son or daughter if they continue the way they are living their life?

The Lord is my light and my salvation
whom shall I fear?
The Lord is the stronghold of my life
of whom shall I be afraid?
(Ps. 27:1)

Chapter 13

Afraid to Run

David pulled Barbara up off the floor. She was trying to talk to him, trying to calm him. She said, "David, think of what you are doing." Again, he kept saying, "Shut up, shut up." She was filled with panic. She could see David's temper was increasing each moment.

They fought their way into the living room, and he sat her down on a love seat. He took his shirt off and said in a rough voice, "I've got to tie you up." Barbara felt dizzy. She was in such a state of disbelief she could hardly breathe and could hear her heart beat.

The whole time he was talking, it was like it was not even David. She continued to try to talk rationally to him. This person was a stranger who looked somewhat like her son but was not him.

David was the kind of person who would stop you if you were going to kill a bug. For him to harm her in any way was so out of character for him. It seemed this was someone other than her son. He said he had to tie her up and told her to put her hands together. He wrapped his shirt around her hands and neck.

He was not tying her up tightly. It was loose. He said in that same tough voice, "You sit right there." He went into the hall and opened the linen closet to get a towel. She had no idea what he was going to do with it.

As soon as he left her, Barbara was able to remove her hands from the shirt. The sliding glass door going onto her patio was across from her. She felt she had to get away so she ran to the door. She had to unlock the door, but the screen door was locked as well. She made it outside, but by that time, David was right there behind her.

She ran onto the patio screaming. Barbara's neighbors never heard her. He threw his hand over her face. They were struggling, and she bit his finger as hard as she could. That was the last thing Barbara remembers. When she woke up, she was on the floor back in the living room.

David was sitting in a chair, crying. Barbara had no idea how long she had been unconscious. Her head was bleeding, and her body hurting. She was very aware that she needed to keep her composure as though someone was saying to her "stay calm."

Barbara's knees were burning and her head bleeding. David had dragged her into the house from the patio. Her knees had burns from his pulling her across the concrete and then across the carpet. As she was starting to wake up, she put her hand up to her head. David was crying and said, "Oh, I thought you were dead."

Barbara said, "I'm okay, David. I'm okay."

"No you're not. You are bleeding. Your head is bleeding." She didn't want him to become more agitated, so she kept insisting she was fine and would be okay. David said, "I almost killed you. I pounded your head against the cement, and I thought I killed you." He was talking fast and was very distressed.

She asked him to get her some ice to put on her head. David went into the kitchen to get ice. Barbara continued to try and stay calm. She could not believe he pounded her head on the cement until she was unconscious. She really didn't know how much time had gone by.

David began talking about himself. He told her he had never had a bad drug trip or any bad experience on drugs, which she knew was not true. He told her how much he hated his father, and he really had wanted to kill him. He said he had come to the house to get guns from Bob's gun cabinet because he had planned to kill himself and thought he would kill her too. His tone was so matter-of-fact and without emotion.

David said, "You should never have given birth to me and should never have had a child by that man [his dad]." He had such anger against his father. He decided since his dad was in Saudi Arabia, she was the one he was going to kill.

This Was No Longer David

Barbara was in shock and couldn't think what to do but was going moment by moment. She told him she was thirsty, and he let her go into the kitchen to get a drink. She could have run out the door. Later, she played this back in her mind many times and realized she was afraid to try to run. She felt lucky to be alive and didn't want him to attack her again. Barbara knew this was still an explosive situation.

The telephone rang. David had been a little calmer up until then, but when the phone rang, it upset him. He began to be agitated again and told her not to answer it. The anger in him would suddenly erupt. Barbara told him, "People know I am home, and I need to answer."

He said in a tough voice, "Don't you say anything," and he stood right by her.

Barbara's mother-in-law was calling to see how she was feeling. Barbara told her "not so good." Her mother-in-law knew she had the flu, and since she wasn't saying much, she said, "Well, I hope you feel better." When Barbara hung up the phone she thought, "*What should I have said? Should I have said, Help, call the police?*"

Barbara began to think how she was going to get out of this situation, or if she was going to get out of it? David was getting more and more disturbed. She desperately fought against panic.

He said, "What is Bob going to say?"

"I will tell Bob I hit my head on the cupboard."

"He won't believe you."

She tried to convince him Bob would believe her. David began to talk. It was true confession time. He talked and talked. He told her a lot of things he had done. He told her why he had gotten into drugs and how fast he had become addicted to LSD.

As the morning moved along, Barbara remembered her friend was coming over to help her bleach her hair at noon. She was thinking, how can I get David to let her come? She told David her friend, Char, was coming over to bleach her hair. He did not want this.

She reminded him he had met Char once, but no, he did not want her coming! She kept talking to him and saying he could come into the kitchen while they were doing her hair, and she would not say anything. To her surprise, he agreed.

Barbara was a mess. She had been bleeding, and there was blood on both her robe and hair. Just before noon she told him she had to get her jeans on and get these other clothes off. He did not want her to get away from him, so he went into her bedroom with her. She did not feel comfortable as she had to get her underwear on and her jeans and shirt on while he was there.

She remembers when she passed him in the hall, she almost felt like he was going to attack her. She had such fear now because this was not her son.

Barbara's friend came right at noon. When Barbara opened the door, she gave her friend a look to not say anything. Char was shocked, of course, by how Barbara looked. David was close by.

Barbara's head was still bleeding, and her hair was matted with blood. She put her finger up to her lips, and Char seemed to understand she did not want her to ask anything.

Barbara said, "You remember David, don't you?"

David said hello to her and quickly moved into the next room.

They started to get ready to bleach her hair. Barbara told her she would get the things they needed. Char was looking at Barbara strangely as they went into the kitchen. David went into the den to lie down. Surprisingly, he left them alone.

Barbara went to get towels for her hair and was trying to think what to do. She realized now she put her friend in a really dangerous position. She should never have allowed her to come to the house. She apologized to her later as she did not think about how she was endangering her friend's life by allowing her to be there.

As they walked into the kitchen, she was pointing to Barbara's head. Barbara said something about her hair really needed to be done and appreciated her coming over to help. She went to the drawer to get a piece of paper and pencil. She was shaking so much she could hardly hold the pencil.

It was only then she realized just how afraid she really was. She wrote Bob's phone number down and wrote, "Call Bob and tell him to come alone." Char put it into her pocket. She hurriedly put the bleach on Barbara's hair and put a plastic bag around her head. What a sight Barbara was.

Char went out the front door, and later, Barbara wondered why she didn't go with her? Somehow, she thought if David was calm, everything would be okay. She could sit down and talk rationally to him. Who knows what any of us would do in this situation. You want to believe it isn't really happening, or you think the situation is under control.

Unfortunately, David was not calm. He was getting very antsy, very uptight. He started telling her again how close to death she was. He got down on the floor and started showing her how he had pounded her head on the cement. It was horrible to think of what he had done. He also dragged Barbara back into the house across the cement.

Bob received the phone call from Char as he was coming back from lunch. He threw down the phone and drove home in record time.

Barbara looked up and saw him as he passed the kitchen window. She said, "Oh, Bob is coming." David jumped up and began to panic. Barbara was thinking David is six foot two, a big guy, and Bob was walking in without really knowing what was going on.

Bob came bursting into the living room and took one look at Barbara. He could see how bad things were. David walked past Bob and went back in the den to lie down. Bob asked Barbara, "What happened to you?"

She said, "I hit my head on the cupboard."

"You didn't hit your head on the cupboard!" He went into the den where David was and said, "What happened to your mother?"

David said, using that very strange voice, "Well, she said she hit her head on the cupboard."

Bob was so exasperated. "I'm calling the police."

By this time, Barbara was starting to cry and saying, "Don't call the police." She had severe cuts on her head and was bleeding again. She ran out into the front yard as she felt the need to get out of the house.

David came outside and did the strangest thing. He took her face into his hands, kissed her on the lips, and said in that strange voice, "Thank you, Mother dear." Barbara thought later it was so sickening, so disgusting. She wanted to ask this person, "What did you do with my son?"

Bob came out of the house and picked up a club from the garage. David said, "Oh, a lethal weapon, huh?"

"Yes, and I'm ready to use it."

The police then drove in the driveway, and David walked over and introduced himself. He nicely introduced Bob and his mom and told them, "I guess I am the one you are here for."

When Barbara saw the police put David's hands behind his back and put handcuffs on him, she came completely apart. She became hysterical, and all the emotion from all those hours with David came to the surface.

The police wanted to know what happened. Again, Barbara told them the same thing. She had hit her head on the cupboard. She told me later she didn't know why she said that except she still wanted to protect David.

Bob said, "You tell the truth." Barbara sat there stunned as she could hardly believe what just happened. She finally started telling them everything that happened throughout the day.

Barbara felt almost like she was making it up. It was like a dream you don't wake up from. The police took David to the mental health hospital for observation. He would be held there for seventy-two hours.

Bob took Barbara to the hospital where she needed stitches. Barbara knew the doctor personally, and he told her how fortunate she was to be alive. He knew David and said, "Barbara, you cannot trust David anymore. David is not who you think he is." Later, the judge said the same thing, "Please realize you cannot trust David to not hurt you."

The kind of trauma Barbara had gone through can change a person forever. How many of us have really thought we were about to die? There is a wonderful old hymn that says, "Not my brother nor my sister, but it's me, Oh Lord, standing in the need of prayer."[5]

This was where Barbara was. She had prayed for others many times, but right now, she was saying, It's me, oh Lord, standing in the need of prayer.

Questions to Ponder

1. Do you feel your son or daughter could be violent?

2. Are you standing in the need of prayer right now? Do you have Christian friends you can call on to pray with you?

> *I sought the Lord,*
> *and he answered me;*
> *He delivered me*
> *from all my fears.*
> *(Ps. 34:4)*

Chapter 14

Living in Fear

The next four months were torture for Barbara. David was put into a mental hospital where he would not cooperate. He was up and down. She and Bob were able to get him into a Christian drug abuse center at one time, but he refused to do the things they expected of him.

Barbara lived in total fear and anxiety. She would come home, open the door carefully, and look all around. She prayed God would take this fear from her. Even at the library where she worked, she wondered, "If David comes walking in the door, what should I do?"

She could not believe it had come to this. She was so fearful of her own son. She did not really want to see him, but she did talk to him on the phone. She told him they were praying for him.

David had now been in and out of many different facilities. It seemed no matter what they tried, he refused the help he needed. Once when he was not in a facility, David slit his wrists and later walked up to a policeman and told him, "I think you need to take me to the state mental hospital." Barbara's heart hurt for him as she knew he was in pain. She felt the weight of the world on her shoulders.

David did not realize once you put yourself into the state hospital, you cannot just check yourself out. There were procedures. A person cannot decide to stay for a week or two and decide to leave.

One day, he called his mom and said, "Mom, I want you to know I have been talking to the chaplain. He gave me a Bible to read, and I am reading it. I realize all those things I have been searching for is right here."

It was everything Barbara wanted to hear. They had tried to help him in every way possible. He was telling her he understood now how she was trying to help him, and he was going to change. It was an answer to everyone's prayers.

Barbara wanted to believe him, but she could not get it out of her mind his previous comments about being able to con anyone. She was not sure if he was trying to con her or not.

She wanted to go visit him for his twenty-first birthday. He told her he did not want them to visit; he was ready to come home. He wanted to prove how much better he was and promised to get a job.

Barbara knew he could not come home. It would be a long time before they could trust him again as she was still fearful. They wanted to know he was truly well.

The day before they were going to see David, Bob and Barbara were having breakfast, and they saw a policeman walking up to their door. It never occurred to her why he was there. Sadly, he told her David had committed suicide. It was such a shock as she always believed he was going to get better in time.

Barbara felt such sorrow. She thought of the suffering David went through the last few years of his life. Her pain was so deep, but mostly, she thought of the pain David must have had to take his own life. Their whole family and all of their friends grieved with her.

She found out later from the chaplain that David really had been reading the Bible. The chaplain and he had been talking, and David was sharing his feelings. She wanted to believe in his drug state of mind or, hopefully, not in a drug state of mind, David accepted Christ into his heart.

There was something very hard for Barbara to admit. She loved David so much, but at the time of David's death, she felt a relief. She certainly was not glad David died, but with his death, she felt the heavy load of fear lifted.

The way David died was by going into the showers at the state mental hospital and tying a plastic bag around his head. He suffocated. It was so tragic. Barbara could not understand how anyone could do this. She could only imagine being able to do such a thing if you were mentally ill or possibly having a lot of drugs in your system at the time.

What a wonderful precious boy David had been. She loved him, and now he was gone. David's last years had been so sad, and his life cut short. I know God loved David as He did my son, Greg, and I pray David is with the Lord today. The depth of the pain and loss was completely beyond comprehension.

There were funeral arrangements to be made. They had to pick out a casket and a marker for his grave. She had to go to the cemetery and pick out a grave site. The day of the funeral, she found herself standing at the grave site of her son, still wondering how such a terrible thing happened. Barbara remembers years of laughter and joy with David, but the last few years overshadowed all the blessed years.

When this kind of tragedy comes into our lives, we have to look to Christ. How can anyone go through what Barbara did without God? What a waste of a young man's life. She grieved and hurt for the loss of her son.

Now Barbara remembers all the wonderful years she had with David. She wants to remember all the good times they had together and all those precious days before her son was caught in this web of drugs.

She is blessed now with her husband Bob, their five children, and beautiful grandchildren. She still has moments, of course, where she misses David. It still hurts when she thinks of what kind of man he could have been before the drugs. He had such wonderful potential.

God has given Barbara the joy and peace she has today. She said, "When I think about sharing my story, I cannot help but think of this old song."

> *Farther along, we'll know all about it*
> *Farther along we'll understand why*
> *Cheer up my brother, Live in the sunshine*
> *We'll understand it all Bye and Bye* [6]

I pray her story will help you who are going through difficulties in your life with your child. God is there for you to give you the strength you need. He is also there to bring joy and peace back into your life.

The Loss of Hope!

David lost hope when he was in the mental hospital. He struggled so long with his addiction and saw no way out. He did not believe in his value on this planet. If Satan takes our hope, he has won the battle.

There was no reason to think David could not have been successful in whatever he wanted to do with his life. However, drugs are like a cancer that attacks your body and destroys your mind. He had the ability to work, earn money, and build a life for himself, but at some point, David lost hope and could no longer imagine his life being normal again.

Barbara also felt a loss of hope at times, but she knew in her heart she could reach out to God. She could find refuge in Christ because she had built her foundation on strong and solid ground.

God will encourage us, even when our common sense tells us there is no reason for hope, because our source of hope and our source of strength are in the Lord.

When the storms of life came, Barbara was able to stand firm against Satan. This storm for her was strong, the wind blew, and the river was raging. Praise God, He had built a bridge for her across that raging river. We do not need to fear what is ahead because God is with us. Jesus is there to intercede for us, and the Holy Spirit is there to guide us.

God took David home when life was too hard for him to go on. I believe the angels opened wide the pearly gates and welcomed David with songs of praise.

Was a drug-addicted life what David wanted? No, David had great dreams and plans for his life as any other young man, and he had the potential to fulfill those dreams, but Satan took that away. One day, David made a bad choice by taking drugs, and this choice led him down this unbelievably dangerous road. Praise God for the good grace of God because David was covered by the blood of Jesus.

God chose David. David was raised in a Christian home by a Christian mother who prayed for him all his life. She prayed for David and all her children from the time they were born, through their adolescent years, and through their teenage years.

She prayed for David through his drug addiction years. God honors the prayers of a wonderful praying mother.

David was not a terrible person. He did not consciously turn his back on God. He made a mistake as a teenager by taking drugs, which totally destroyed his mind.

He loved his mother. He did not want to kill her. He did not want to have this life of pain and mental suffering, nor did he want to kill himself. The drugs took over his thinking. Satan wanted to take his eternal life, but this was not God's plan.

David made mistakes when he was young. The truth is we all do. Each one of us made mistakes in our youth. There are things I did as a teenager, which I am sorry and embarrassed about now, and there were consequences to those mistakes.

If a teenager makes a mistake by driving one hundred miles an hour and is pulled over by the police, he will have consequences. He will pay a very expensive ticket and may get his license taken away. If a teenage girl makes a bad choice by having sex, she may have the bad consequence of being pregnant.

Most all teenagers make mistakes that have consequences; however, most of these mistakes you can deal with and go on in life. It may be a setback, but you can continue life and have many wonderful years ahead of you.

Unfortunately, David's mistake had the most major of consequences. Unlike a traffic fine or pregnancy, David's consequences led to addiction. Addiction then led to his death. Was David's sin any worse than those of others? No, but the consequences were so much greater.

We, as parents, try to teach our children the danger of taking drugs. But who knows which child will give in to the temptation of drugs and who will not. If you raise a child who is continually being rebellious, you might expect this, but David was not a disobedient child.

David was a sweet charming delightful teenager who made a poor decision in judgment, which cost him his life. He was a student body officer and a head drum major. Almost overnight, addiction will take a boy with so much potential and in a relatively short time, his life was ruined.

Does David pay for this teenage mistake with losing eternal life with God? No, our God is a God of love. This could happen to my child or your child as easily as it did David. Barbara fought this for years, but the actual going from a normal boy to a drug addict happened very quickly.

Once David took that first drug, he was no longer the same. When you throw a rock into the lake, the ripples keep widening and touch the lives of everyone around you. David became addicted to drugs, and many ripples went out from there in all areas of his life and his family.

Everyone tried to help David, but it was all in vain. Only God could take away the darkness he was going through. I am so thankful we have a God of mercy, grace, forgiveness and above all, love. God knew David and loved him.

David's life here on earth was short. The angels came for David like a wonderful quiet movement of the wind. God saw and knew the good in David and the beautiful child and young man that he was. Barbara was afraid for him, but David did not belong to Satan. He was a child of God.

God understood David made bad choices and foolish mistakes as a teen, but God loved him more than anyone else could love him. I believe David is at peace now with his Creator. The gates of heaven opened wide to welcome him and the angels sang, "Hallelujah! Hallelujah!"

Questions to Ponder

1. How do you ever stop the pain of losing a child?

2. Are you struggling with a loss of hope? Are you trying to handle life's challenges on your own?

Those who hope in the Lord
Will renew their strength.
They will run and not grow weary,
they will walk and not be faint.
(Isa. 40:31)

Chapter 15

Cling to the
Old Rugged Cross

There is a beautiful song written by Geo Bernard entitled "The Old Rugged Cross"[7] with a line that says, "On a hill far away stood an old rugged cross the emblem of suffering and shame." It is because of that cross we have forgiveness of sins. For a world of lost sinners was slain, that included David.

Another line of the song says, "I will cling to the old rugged cross." Friend, this is what we do as Christians. When we see our children out of control and taking the wrong path, this is the time we cling to the old rugged cross. This is what Barbara did.

David needed to ask the Lord for help, but he was in no state of mind to really be able to think through what was happening to him. Once David was addicted, he could no longer help himself. Praise God David had a praying mother. He had family and friends praying for him.

God is pleased when we turn to Him with our cares. We do not need to carry the weight of the world on our shoulders. Jesus died on the cross for my sins and for your sins. He also died for David's sins. Christ gave His blood for each and every one of us. God knows what the circumstances of our lives are today. He knew David's circumstances.

Praise God for His understanding and mercy! I look forward

to meeting David in heaven and seeing the joy on Barbara's face as she sees her beloved son again.

I feel sad for Barbara's loss but thankful she was willing to share her story with you. There are many parents in pain because of the path their child has taken. This was certainly a testing of Barbara's faith. Could she trust God? Could she trust his promises?

How do we move on after such a terrible tragedy? How does a parent cope with such a loss? How does any parent come to terms with their child dying so young? David's death seemed so senseless.

Get off the Treadmill Of Grief and Sadness

It was a struggle for Barbara, but she found she had more spiritual strength than she would have thought possible. If she would have known such a terrible tragedy was going to happen to her family, she would not have thought she would be able to survive.

When you experience a tragedy, a personal crisis, or a life-changing event, it is perfectly normal to go through stages of denial, fear, anger, sadness, and grief. At some point, however, we must admit to ourselves we have no control over what happened, but we do have control over our future.

The word *grief* is a verb, and the dictionary tells us it is to feel deep emotion of pain and heartache. Grief is something we go through, but we do not want to get stuck in the grief cycle. There is a time to finish grieving and let the healing process begin. When I was grieving for Greg I had to ask God, "Please, Lord, free my heart of this grief and pain."

We cannot understand God's plans, but we know whatever

heartaches we go through, He allows us to go through. We know for sure He loves us with love that is far beyond our ability to comprehend. In the darkness of fear and in the darkness of grief, God's voice can fill you with peace and calm.

The weight of so much happening to Barbara at one time was difficult. It is when you are at your lowest that Satan will come, and he will try to take your peace of mind and your faith. He will sap your energy and strength. Satan's plan is to destroy us.

There are times Barbara might have felt helpless and alone, but God had never left her side. He was there all the time. When we turn to God, His mighty love comes to us stronger than ever. I pray this gives a glimmer of hope to other Christian parents who have lost a child. You can survive with your faith intact.

Do you sometimes feel lost and wonder if anyone cares what you are going through? Jesus loves you with a great and mighty love. He knows the trials and the pressures of life you are facing.

Whatever comes into your life no matter how bad the circumstances, God will not let you down! Through all life's disappointments and heartaches, He is faithful.

Barbara was in turmoil with David. She was watching her son go downhill, but she claimed God's promises. The Bible tells us to not be anxious or worried about anything. We need to go to God in prayer and ask for His peace and a calm spirit.

In Philippians, the Bible says, "We can have the peace of God, which transcends all understanding." Only God can reach down into our hearts to heal our pain. He frees us from suffering, and in Barbara's case, the loss of a child. In time, she was able to accept David's life as a gift even though she had him for a shorter time than she would have liked.

We see our present situations in light of our understanding of our world. God looks at our lives and the lives of our children in view of eternity.

GOD'S LOAN

"I'll lend to you for a little time,
A child of mine, He said,
For you to love the while he lives
And mourn for when he's dead.

It may be six or seven years
Or twenty-two or three,
But will you till I call him back,
Take care of him for me?

He'll bring his charms to gladden you
And should his stay be brief,
You'll have these precious memories,
As solace for your grief.

I cannot promise he will stay
Since all from earth return.
But there are lessons taught down there
I want this child to learn.

I've looked this whole world over,
In my search for teachers true.
And in the crowds that throng life's land,
I have selected you. (Barbara)

Now will you give him all your love
Not think the labor vain,
Nor hate me when I come to call
To take him back again?

It seems to me I heard them say,
Dear Lord, Thy will be done.
For all the joys thy child shall bring,
The risk of grief we'll run."

"We'll shelter him with tenderness,
We'll love him while we may,
And for the happiness we've known
Forever grateful stay.

And should the angels call for him
Much sooner than we've planned,
We'll brave the bitter grief that comes
And try to understand."[8]

Our Life's Journey

During our life's journey, there will be storms of life that come. There can be valleys we must go through of darkness, depression and despair, accidents, loss of finances, insecurity, loss of loved ones, loneliness, heartbreak, personal pain, a spouse leaving, or fear of the future. The list can go on and on.

As you put your trust in God, you may find He has a very different plan for you and your adult child. It could be a plan much different than you could ever envision. It is through the power of believing God wants what is best for us that helps us to be able to put our lives in His hands.

If you are going through difficult times, God is there to give you peace. God can heal you or your loved one of illness. God can heal and repair your broken heart. God can lift your spirits in time of despair. God can restore your soul.

He does not want you to stay in this sorrow for what has happened in your life. When discouragement and despair comes to your mind, just whisper the name of Jesus. God wants you to be full of joy and happiness here on earth. His spirit will free you from a tragedy so you are able to enjoy life again.

They say to everything there is a season. Winter, spring, summer, and fall seasons come and go just as the seasons of our lives come and go. There are seasons of our life that change us as with Barbara. Her child was gone. In life you may be overwhelmed with sadness and your heart damaged. God knows and is not surprised by what is happening. This is a "season" in your life.

When Driving Your Car Forward You cannot be Looking Backward

It's the Same in Life

Leave the Past Behind And Look Forward To God's Blessings!

Life here on earth will begin and end. Where will your journey take you between the beginning and the end of your life? Is Christ with you on your journey? I am thankful and blessed to have Christ always with me throughout my life.

This may be the end of a season for you and the beginning of a new chapter in your life. Just as the flowers die out in the winter, spring comes, and they bloom again as beautiful as ever. Your life is not over. Your happy days are not gone. Yes, there is sadness, but there is an excitement of what God has planned for you.

If there are mistakes you have made in the past, you have to forgive yourself. If others have hurt you deeply, it is time to forgive them and go forward. Do not continue looking back on difficult times, but look forward to the new plan that God has for you.

There was so much I did not understand regarding the *why* of what happened to Greg. Knowing God is in control helps to make more sense out of tragedy.

I pray this book will help to heal the broken hearts of moms who have lost hope. Your unbelievable sadness can turn to peace and happiness again. It is God's love that will fill you with peace and joy.

The last three chapters of this book are written to help you find peace and joy.

Questions to Ponder

1. Do you think God wants you to go through the remainder of your life with grief and sadness, because of your child's choices in life?

2. If your wayward child continues on their destructive path, are you ready to receive peace for yourself?

Trust in the Lord with all your heart and
lean not on your own understanding;
In all your ways submit to him,
And He will direct your paths.
(Prov. 3: 5-6a)

Part Four

The Courage to
Take Your Life Back

Chapter 16

The Road to Recovery

How do we find peace and joy when we are in the midst of despair? How do we remain calm when we see our son or daughter self-destructing before our very eyes?

I encourage you as a parent to take your life back and move on from continual heartbreak. There is a Road to Recovery from despair; however, it takes discipline and focus. Tragedies in life happen to the Christian and the non-Christian equally.

None of us know what life has in store for us. We all walk unknown paths. We are all vulnerable to life's unexpected and unforeseen challenges. It may not be an adult child you are dealing with, but other kinds of challenges causing you emotional pain.

Possibly, you have had a financial disaster, which has turned your life upside down. Do you feel lost in loneliness? Are you facing divorce and feeling forsaken and rejected? Are you struggling with a physical illness? Have you lost a spouse? Are you fighting depression?

You can have true peace and joy regardless of the circumstances you find yourself in. If you are in prison you can find joy. If you are in a loveless marriage you can find joy. Throughout our lives, we will have to walk paths of uncertainty. These changes in our lives are sometimes unwelcomed.

Our greatest challenges in life can be to adjust to a new lifestyle we didn't choose. Story after story shows us it is through faith in God we receive the energy and the fortitude we need to carry on.

All three of these young men had great hopes and dreams as they were growing up. They were raised in good Christian homes. What happened? Greg had the tragedy of being bipolar and spending time in a penitentiary. Jason's challenges were being homosexual and then sudden death. David faced drug addiction and death.

Tragedy can leave a scar on our heart and wound us in a way in which a parent can be hurt for all of their lives. This is not God's plan for you.

God has prepared the way for us through these highs and lows. We can stop agonizing and worrying about our children and put our trust in Him. "Therefore, do not worry about tomorrow, for tomorrow will worry about itself. Each day has enough trouble of its own." (Matt. 6:34)

Before starting the Road to Recovery, let's evaluate if you are ready to separate yourself from the discouraging path your adult child has taken. Ask yourself these questions.

1. Are you ready to accept that the responsibility of your child's bad choices and the consequences of those choices lie wholly on their shoulders?
2. Are you ready to stop beating yourself up and feeling guilty for their actions?
3. Are you ready to accept it is only God and He alone who can reach into the heart of your child and He alone who can turn them from their destructive lifestyle?
4. Are you ready to *let go* and stop allowing your child to continue to hurt and destroy you?

5. Are you ready to take the focus off of your child and begin to plan how you can enjoy your life again?

6. Are you ready to accept there is a chance your son or daughter may never change their path of self-destruction in your lifetime?

7. Are you ready to learn how to live a life of happiness in spite of the fact your child continues down that slippery slope?

8. Are you ready to totally and completely turn their lives over to Jesus?

If so, God is asking you to take that first step. We have a speedy calendar, and the days and the months slip by quickly. Now is the day to start, not next week or next month.

Many of us wish our adult children would make better decisions. *Now it is time for you to make a better decision.* This decision may be to change how you are dealing with your son or daughter.

In this Road to Recovery, I have three steps to help you be released from the crushing heartache you have watching your child heading down the wrong path. You will be able to trust God more and move on with happiness in your life. This plan requires *ACTION* on your part.

Three Step Plan

1. **Stop enabling**
2. **Let go of the pain**
3. **Spiritual growth**

Step 1 - Stop Enabling – Take Action

You have been trying to help your adult child possibly for years. When you think you have done all you can possibly do, you probably have.

You can see from these three stories the parents did everything they could think to do. They tried all they could to help their sons, to no avail. If you find yourself in this place, I can relate.

Our wayward adult children do not take our advice and eventually resent us when we try to help them. It is hard to admit, but at some point, we become enablers.

The hardest and most difficult thing for a parent to do is to *stop helping*. Especially for moms, as we are always trying to fix things, including our children. Have you fallen into the trap of enabling? See if any of these circumstances sound familiar to you.

1. You help them with money telling them and yourself this is the last time.
2. You help them get their car fixed. Of course, they need help. How can they go to work or how do they even look for a job without a car?
3. Babysit the grandchildren again? I am really too tired, but yes, I will baby sit them again.
4. You suggest a job you heard about, thinking they may be interested.
5. You see them being lazy so you choose your words carefully to get them motivated.
6. You tell them, we are happy you found the right person, but maybe you should not get married so quickly. Give it a little more time! They don't listen.

7. You see they are being irresponsible, so you try to give them easy and practical things to do.
8. You let them move back in with you for a "temporary" time period. They are still there.
9. You think they are breaking the law so you try talking to them about the serious consequences they may face.
10. You pray some more.
11. After six months, you tell them nicely I think it is time you find your own place. They are still there.
12. You try talking to them about drinking and suggest they go to AA. You offer to go with them.
13. You have a serious conversation about the consequences of their drug addiction.
14. You suggest counseling may help. You offer to pay for counseling.
15. You give them financial advice you know would really benefit them, if they would only listen.
16. You pray, pray, pray.

Sound familiar?

We can try to help in every way—help with money, help get their car fixed, try to get them off drugs, and the list goes on. I believe it takes a miracle for a parent to be able to stop worrying, losing sleep, and turn this completely and totally over to God. Praying is by far the most important and sometimes the only thing you can do.

Our Adult Children

They ask our advice
We give them advice
They don't take it!

**They don't ask
our advice
We give it anyway
They still don't take
it!**

**Bottom Line:
Stop Giving
Unwanted Advice!**

Even when we know in our heart there is nothing more we can do, we try again, but see no change in our son or daughter. Why do we keep putting ourselves through this? The answer is, of course, because we love them and our heart continually tells us we can help.

Maybe you have heard the saying, "Don't try to teach a pig to sing. It just annoys the pig and frustrates you!" In other words, stop enabling. It does not work.

If we have a financial disaster which we are unable to recover from, or if we learn we have an incurable disease, it is easier for us to accept that the situation is now "out of our control."

It is harder to come to this conclusion when we are dealing with our children. The situation is out of our control but we continue to try to help when we really need to accept the fact we have done all we can.

There are boundaries to what we can do and there are times when we can no longer help. We waste precious energy continuing to try to change them.

Some parents might say, "You don't understand. My child is unable to take care of himself. He is emotionally and mentally incapable of making correct decisions." This is usually not the case. But even if it is true; they must learn to adapt to whatever their challenges are. You can help them but only if they are willing to take the steps necessary to become independent of you.

Sadly, you may be a parent who has a child living in the street or sleeping in a car. This makes the daily suffering and sorrow even more intense. It does not change the facts of what you as a parent can and cannot do. They may need to get more desperate before they are willing to seek help.

We want to let our child know we love and accept them. Be

there to encourage? Yes. Be there to listen? Yes. It is difficult but important to stop with the advice they don't ask for which they won't take anyway. Stop loaning money they will not pay back.

If there are grandchildren involved, invest your time and energy in them. You can buy clothes for them, take them to special events, pay for them to play a sport, and give them special attention. Allow mom and dad to figure out *their own lives*. You have to stop your own destructive cycle of enabling. How can they become responsible adults if you always save them?

If you want the insanity and chaos to stop, start today by putting all your efforts into prayer. We never stop loving our children, but we have our own lives to live. God does not want you to live a life of despair because of your adult child's actions.

Do not let Satan control the situation and hurt you any longer. In my story, I had to turn it over to God each and every morning. I put a sign on my medicine cabinet which said, "God, I will turn this over to you *again* today!"

There is sadness when we see our adult child making bad choices, but sadness is not something God wants for your life. You need refreshing. There is a song I love which has a line, "There is a river of life flowing from deep within." What does this mean? Where does this river come from?

When feeling overwhelmed and burdened over your child, a fountain of love is flowing directly from God to you. The river of life flows from heaven to us giving us peace and calm.

You may see a wonderful answer to prayer and see your child make a detour from the wrong path back to the right path. Praise God, this is what we pray for and hope for. However, we may not see this change in our lifetime. This is where we show total faith in God. I choose to have faith whatever circumstances come my way. I may not understand but I trust God.

In this sinful world, we will get beat up, knocked down, be heartbroken, and face many trials. This is why it is important to really understand what the word *faith* means. Faith is more than believing wholeheartedly that all will work itself out. It is not "whatever will be, will be."

The dictionary tells us faith is having confidence in something, assurance and conviction. An even better explanation of faith is what the Bible says. "Faith is being sure of what we hope for and certain of what we do not see." (Heb. 11:1) Faith is what you believe for in prayer. Praying for something you have *not* received. It is something you desire and hope for. If you already received it, *there is no reason to have faith.*

There are times when we pray and do not receive the answer we were hoping for. Remember God sees the bigger picture. There were also times I felt God had not answered my prayers, but I later realized He just didn't answer in my time frame. Remember, when your plans do not work out as you hoped, it is because He has a different and better plan for you.

> *For my thoughts are not your thoughts,*
> *neither are your ways my ways,*
> *declares the Lord.*
> *As the heavens are higher than the earth,*
> *so are my ways higher than your ways*
> *and my thoughts than your thoughts.*
> *(Isa. 55:8-9)*

God has entrusted us with these precious children. We have a responsibility as parents to raise them to know God and teach them about Jesus. This in itself does not give us any guarantees of how our children behave as adults.

Some parents are neglectful and have not been good parents, but I knew I had been a good parent and raised my children with good values. I had to stop feeling guilty, and I was only able to do that with God's help.

We can be assured if we do our part raising our children with prayer, God will not fail us. If you did not raise your child in this way, begin today praying for them, and God will honor your faithfulness.

Dealing with the challenges sent our way, you can be broken, bitter, and depressed. Sometimes, it feels there is no one who could possibly understand how you are feeling, but God understands. He understands and will see you through these dark times.

Your journey may not be as dramatic as the stories of these three young men, but your pain and suffering is equal.

God desires to give you peace and joy starting today. At the time I was going through the roller coaster of emotions with Greg, God gave me this verse that expresses what I have tried to impart throughout the entire book.

When you pass through the waters,
I will be with you.
And when you pass through the rivers,
they will not sweep over you.
When you walk through the fire,
you will not be burned;
the flames will not set you ablaze.
For I am the Lord your God.
(Isa. 43:2)

Wow! I walked through the fire and was not burned! The flames did not set me a blaze! Thank you, Lord!

Step One Action

1. How might you be enabling your son or daughter? Ask God to help you release them to Him.
2. Memorize Isa. 43:2. It will carry you through many challenges throughout your life.

I repeat it here.

> *When you pass through the waters,*
> *I will be with you.*
> *And when you pass through the rivers,*
> *they will not sweep over you.*
> *When you walk through the fire,*
> *you will not be burned;*
> *the flames will not set you ablaze.*
> *For I am the Lord your God.*
> *(Isa. 43:2)*

Chapter 17

Letting Go of the Pain, But How?

If your child does not change their ways, of course this brings heartache. You may worry about them day and night. You may be thinking, "I want to turn over all my frustrations to Jesus and trust Him. I want peace and joy instead of the continual turmoil and chaos in my life, but how?"

Step 2 – Letting go of the Pain – Take Action

When a Child Keeps Hurting You

Some questions to consider:

1. How long have you been suffering because of your child's actions?
2. How long have you been dealing with this chaotic lifestyle your adult child causes?
3. Do you feel your son or daughter sometimes tries to hurt you?
4. Is it affecting other members of your family?
5. How does it affect your spouse?

You are the one who has to break the cycle of grief and pain not your son or daughter. You need a plan of action. Without a plan of action you will wake up tomorrow doing the same thing you have been doing and expect the outcome to be different. The outcome will be the same!

Be prepared for the next crisis your child brings into your life. You know it will come. Will it be asking for money? Will it be asking to crash at your house? Will it be showing up at your door drunk? Will it be a comment to hurt you or make you feel guilty? Will it be a complaint of their childhood? Will it be a slur of cussing? Will it be a phone call in which you know they are high on something? It may be as simple as them being disrespectful and condescending.

This is where you need to be prepared. Think through each possible scenario so you will know exactly what you will say or do. Most importantly; do not enable them in any way.

It is time to let your child fly solo whether he or she is twenty-five years old or forty-five years old. You are not releasing your child into the world and its sinful ways, but you are *releasing them to God!*

Your adult child must accept responsibility and accountability for the lifestyle he or she has chosen. You are not responsible. They are. Let go and work on getting your life back to normal and do not let your child's drama destroy you. You *can* put your shattered heart back together with God's help.

Your outlook on life can change in the midst of difficulties. God can help you to control your emotions when dealing with adversity. If you ask God, He will help you change your attitude and how you respond to your child's new crisis.

Adjust your thoughts on what you can and cannot do. Shift your focus from the difficult child back to yourself and other members of your family. Often times, our other children, even if they are adults, begin to feel forgotten. Are you investing the same amount of time and prayer to your other children?

When you really turn these challenges over to God, you will see what wonderful blessings He has for you. Allow that heavy burden, that load of suffering, and that continual drama to be lifted off you. God doesn't want you to spend the rest of your life, or even one more day in depression or despair.

> *"For I know the plans I have for you,*
> *declares the Lord, plans to prosper you*
> *and not to harm you, plans to give you*
> *hope and a future." (Jer. 29:11)*

Mudslide into Depression

In order to let go of the pain you are feeling it is important to be aware that overwhelming challenges can cause a person to spiral into depression.

We see in the news stories of mudslides happening in different parts of the world. I cannot imagine how frightening it would be if the mountainside behind my house started sliding. There is no stopping it. It may take out a group of homes or a whole village.

Because I lived in Southern California for many years, I can tell you mudslides are a serious problem. We see the videos of houses and personal possessions being carried down the hills.

It must be heart-wrenching to see the mud carrying away your pictures, furniture, and memories. The owner is, of course, thankful to be alive, but the loss is enormous.

What causes the mudslide? The rain comes, and the ground becomes saturated. The mud gets so heavy the weight can no longer hold back the hill, and as it begins to move, it destroys everything in its path.

This can happen in our hearts as well. Problems that come into our lives can bring depression and sorrow. Add to it loss of hope and negative thinking and before you know it, you find a mudslide of despair building up until it is so heavy it can destroy your faith. This will weigh our hearts down and as the heaviness of our heart grows, it picks up weight and speed and takes us down into depression.

If you feel you are falling into the hole of depression; stop what is happening before you go too far down that road. Your struggles are an opportunity for growth and maturing in your Christian walk.

The Bible does not say, "If we face trials, but it says *when* we face trials." Trials and challenges in our lives will build our character. We can turn our hardships into times of spiritual growth.

We can choose how to respond to what happens in our lives. Will we respond in a negative way or a positive way? Take time to reevaluate the choices you make. You make hundreds of choices each day.

When you wake up each morning you can:

- Choose to be happy or choose to be sad.
- Choose to eat oatmeal or choose to eat eggs.
- Choose to go to work or choose to stay home.
- Choose to go to college or choose to learn a trade.
- Choose to read your Bible or choose to watch TV.
- Choose to eat fattening food or choose to eat healthy.
- Choose to exercise or choose to sleep in.

- Choose to loan money to your child or choose to say no.
- Choose to worry about your adult child or choose to trust God.

In order to let go of the pain, we can choose to be happy and not sad. We can choose to turn these problems over to God and stop worrying and hurting. These are steps of *ACTION*.

I heard an interesting comment on TV one day. An older gentleman was talking about his country, India. I have been to India and will never forget the hard life the people who live there endure. Millions of people live in lean to shacks in slum areas. They have little to eat and search for food in garbage dumps. The person being interviewed was a very poor elderly man who was expressing his feelings on life. He said, "I wake up every morning with an explosion of joy for life!"

Wake up every morning with an Explosion of Joy For Life!

How amazing he can feel this way when to you or I, it would seem his life would be a miserable existence, but he had an amazing outlook on life. He was able to dwell on the wonderful blessings he had been given.

Do not dwell on the negative. Look at your life through different colored glasses. It is easy to fall into depression when you feel life is not treating you fairly. We have a beautiful life to enjoy regardless of how bad the problems are that come our way. We can have an explosion of joy every morning like this gentleman from India.

There is so much to be thankful for and God has given us so much beauty to behold. God speaks to us not only through his Word but through creation. Where does the rainbow come from? What makes the rose bud open? There are beautiful sunsets to enjoy. The star filled sky on a wonderful evening. It is amazing to see one hundred tulips growing on the road side. The Canadian Rockies are awesome to see.

God's creations are beautiful and astounding. Why does the giraffe have such a long neck? Have you seen the birth of a baby goat? What a sight it is to see a herd of zebra running. It is beautiful to see the pink flamingo and the white swan. There is so much to enjoy but sometimes we let the hardships of life destroy us from enjoying the beauty of life.

Happiness versus Peace and Joy

I read on a billboard once, "He who dies with the most toys, wins!" What? What kind of foolish and misguided person would write this on a billboard? However, I am sure there are many people who think this is what happiness is all about.

Happiness has nothing to do with possessions or status in life. Every day, we see wealthy people unhappy, and we also see people who have very little enjoying life to the fullest. There are people who have everything a person could possibly want— beautiful homes, large bank accounts, success, lots of attention—and none of this brought them happiness.

Happiness is not the same as peace and joy. Peace and joy only come from the Lord. You cannot buy peace or joy on eBay. We can have joy whether we are going through wonderful days or difficult circumstances. It is only through Christ our Savior that we receive peace and joy which reaches down to our soul.

Our journey in life will not always be smooth sailing. It

may take us through mountain highs and valley lows. It will take us down paths of uncertain outcome, but it is a wonderful and fascinating journey.

Yes, there are adversities along the way, but with God in charge of our lives, we can come through any and all trials and dwell on the beauty and blessings He sends our way. When life's struggles come, you can find a safe retreat in Christ. You can renew yourself in His presence when thinking on His many blessings.

Barbara, Beth, and I are all mothers who went through great tragedies. The struggles our sons went through are something that you would never imagine would happen to your child. God loved Greg, Jason and David. We thank Him for the life they had and the joy they gave us. Through God's grace and love, we moms were able to overcome unbelievable heartache and find peace.

If you saw me during the time our nineteen-year-old son was going to a penitentiary, you would not always see a positive person trusting God. Our human emotions sometimes take over. I know Barbara and Beth would agree. Each day your emotions can rise and fall, but we are now stronger because of what we endured.

In the midst of problems and crisis, in the midst of my faults and failures, in the midst of my lack of faith, I prayed, "Lord, help me to trust you more. Build my faith and give me peace."

How can I have a song in my heart? How can I have a skip in my step? How did Barbara and Beth find happiness, peace, and joy after the loss of their sons? Jesus! He gives us a song in our hearts and gives us pure and authentic joy. The most difficult challenges in life do not dampen our excitement of walking with our Savior.

We can all find things to be unhappy about, but don't be that person. Be the person who finds something to smile about each day. You can find pleasure in the moment and praise God each day while going through difficult times.

Research tells us that we have about 50,000 thoughts in a day! Are they good thoughts? If your thoughts are full of grumbling and discontent; this is a sign of what is in your heart. When negative thoughts come to mind, take control and turn those thoughts to praise. Memorize scripture or write out a scripture for the week you can carry with you.

Each day of our life is a gift. Don't waste it on worry and regrets. You can control your attitude, and you can control your thinking. God gives us a pathway to walk, and along that path are markers to show us the way. Pay attention! Hear His voice!

The reason we have stop signs on our roads and highways is to warn us of potential danger. There are signs to remind us to slow down. It is wise for us to heed these warnings. These signs warn us if we do not stop at the stop sign, there is danger.

God also gives us stop signs in life. He is trying to warn us. Do you sometimes hear that still small voice in your heart? This is God. He may want you to take a different road than you are on. He may want you to turn around and go in the opposite direction.

I look back at my heartache with Greg and think how much easier it would have been if I would have trusted God all along. Life's problems are not so heavy, if we let God help us carry the load.

I am embarrassed to say while I was going through my suffering with Greg, there were times I fretted. I worried. I cried and lost sleep. I was consumed at times thinking about him.

This is human nature for all of us. It is self-destructive to continually worry about the outcome of your circumstances.

This does not sound like what I have been writing in this book. I had to learn to trust God and put my faith in Him. I did grow in my faith through our tragedy. I knew I had to take control of my thinking patterns and stop negative thinking. This took *ACTION* on my part.

If you are not a Christian, giving your heart to God through accepting Jesus Christ as your Savior is the most important thing you can do. If you do not know Christ, you can meet Him now. If you have wandered away from the Lord, He is calling you back right this moment.

When Jesus died on the cross, He paid the price for our sins that we might be forgiven and have eternal life through faith in Him. If you are a Christian and feel your soul is dry, God wants to refresh you.

God loves you with an everlasting love. Having a relationship with Jesus Christ is what gives us hope for the future and strength for today. "For God so loved the world that He gave His one and only Son, that whoever believes in Him shall not perish but have eternal life." (John 3:16)

If you would like to accept Jesus into your heart, ask Him today.

> *Lord Jesus,*
> *I believe You are the Son of God and You died*
> *for me. Please come into my heart and be my*
> *Lord and Savior. I ask You to forgive me for all*
> *my sins and cleanse me with Your precious blood.*

Take control of every area of my life from this moment on.

Jesus, fill me with Your Holy Spirit and empower me to be used for Your glory. I will serve You, love You, and obey You all the days of my life. Thank You for making me Your child. Amen!

Step Two Action

1. Re-evaluate the choices you make each day in regards to your adult child. Consider how you will *respond differently* to them. Write out some possible scenarios.

2. Exchange depression for happiness. Thank God for His many blessings. What can you do today to bring happiness into your life?

There is a time for everything and a
season for every activity under heaven.
A time to weep and a time to laugh
A time to mourn and a time to dance
A time to embrace and a time to refrain
(Eccl. 3:1,4,5b)

Chapter 18

Spiritual Growth

S tep Three of the Road to Recovery will help you be the person God wants you to be. Following my Spiritual Growth plan will help you begin building your mind and heart on a solid foundation. When trials come, you will be ready! We as Christians can always learn to be more faithful.

Step 3 - Spiritual Growth —Take Action

It is an easy program, however, it takes discipline. I think these are two important questions to ask yourself.

How can we expect God to answer our prayers if we have no relationship with Him? How can we ask God to intervene in our child's life if we have no time for Him in our own life?

Sometimes, it is the most important things in life we give the least attention to, such as spiritual growth. We often get sidetracked with busyness. Where are your priorities? How much time or importance is God in your life? If we are not careful, we will overcrowd our lives and leave little room for God.

We find ourselves thinking about where we will go on our next vacation. We need a newer car. Our children are starting school. I want to buy a house. I'm going to plan a BBQ. On and on, we plan.

All is good, then you get a phone call, and you go from

happy-go-lucky to this unbelievable news that changes your life forever. All other plans come to a complete halt when tragedy hits your family, and we find we have to reevaluate life's priorities. My first thought when tragedy hit our family was, *I need to talk to God!*

God, Do You Text?

There are so many ways we can communicate with others. The encyclopedia explains we can communicate by letter, electronic mail, newspaper, books, magazines, radio, proclamation, broadcast, dispatch, radio, telecast, telephone, telegram, computer, cable, radiogram, circulate papers, notes, memorandums, mass media, satellite, radar, dictaphone, loud speaker, walkie-talkie, ship to shore, drawings, paintings, advertisements, post cards, posters, tablets, and, of course, Twitter, Facebook, and Texting!

Isn't it wonderful we do not have to communicate with God in this way? We can quiet our hearts and speak to God whenever and wherever we are. We are not put on hold. We do not need to push 1 for one department and 2 for something else. We are not talking to someone who is in another country and speaks little English.

Thank you, God. You made it so easy for us. We do not have to go through any electronic device to talk with our Heavenly Father. If we want a closer relationship with God, we will need to spend time with Him. We must patiently wait for God's guidance.

Having a conversation with God should be a two-way conversation, not just us doing all the talking. Often when God wants to speak to us, we are up and off to our busy day.

When a farmer plants seed, he must wait for the land to

yield its valuable crop. He must be patient. He waits for the rain to come and help the grain grow. He waits for the sun to come out at just the right time as too much sun can dry out and kill the seed. The weeds need to be pulled and the plants need to be fertilized.

The farmer does all he can and then waits patiently. One morning, he sees the small growth first. In another week or two, he sees more growth. Each day, his seed grows and becomes stronger. He goes to check his crop one morning, and it is ready for harvest. He will have a successful crop, but he had to have patience.

In your spiritual walk with God we start very much the same way. We plant the seed of spiritual growth and grow with commitment. As you learn more of God and step out in faith, your spiritual life develops.

When starting an exercise program to get in shape physically, we start slow. We don't start by lifting the heaviest weights to build our muscles. We start slow using light weights and add more weight as our muscles develop. We build our muscles with constant and continual exercise.

You can grow emotionally as well. Our emotions do not need to be up and down depending on the circumstances of the day. Control of our emotions can grow as they are linked to our spiritual growth. God desires we continue to develop and mature in our walk with Him. He doesn't want to be a *guest* in your home. He wants to live in your heart daily.

There are seven elements of spiritual growth in our plan of *ACTION*. I have a chart at the end of the chapter for you to follow your progress. If you follow the chart, it will help you see where you can put more effort into your walk with the

Lord. I believe you will see a wonderful change in your relationship with Christ.

Small changes in our daily routine can make big changes in our lives. We have been reading about our adult children making bad choices. Now it may be time for you to consider your own choices. God is asking you to choose which fork in the road you will take.

The whole idea of growing spiritually is not going to change your adult child. It is to change you. It is to help you be so strong in your Christian walk that nothing in life rattles you. It will help you be strong spiritually and be filled with peace and joy.

Devotions are the most important thing you can do to jumpstart your spiritual journey. I have broken devotions down into three phases—reading God's Word, prayer, and praise.

When you have devotions, you are saying to God, "I will take time from my day to be with you and you alone." We have twenty-four hours a day. Can we not take time to read the Bible, to praise God, and thank Him for his blessings? We make choices each day of how busy we will be that day. Are you allowing enough time for God in your life?

Many who are reading this book have been Christians for a long time. However, I believe you also will receive blessings from my Spiritual Growth plan. God may speak to your heart showing you ways you could be more faithful to Him.

Seven Elements of Spiritual Growth

1. Reading God's Word

Do you want to know what God's will is for your life? God speaks to us through His Word. To grow deeper in the knowledge of who Jesus is, we begin by reading and studying His Word. It never ceases to amaze me when I am reading my Bible faithfully, God speaks! He speaks not just to anyone but to me. He speaks specifically to me!

Read his Word and ask him to show you how to obey his will. "Your word is a lamp to my feet and a light for my path." (Ps.119:105) God tells us He will give us light for our path.

In the book of James we are told to be doers of the word, and not hearers only. We not only read the Bible, but we need to absorb it.

When you have a rash such as poison ivy, you buy medication to help it heal. The medication only works after you apply it. The Bible has commandments, encouragement, guidance, examples, and lessons. When we read God's Word, we need to apply it to our lives for it to be useful.

Start reading your Bible faithfully. I like the New International Version (NIV) for new Christians. I find The Life Application Study Bible to be refreshing as it helps us know how to apply what we are reading to our everyday lives. It gives fresh insight and makes what we are reading relevant for today. There are also wonderful devotional books especially written for women to strengthen our walk with the Lord.

2. Prayer

The Bible tells us the prayers of a righteous man are powerful. I have experienced the incredible power of prayer! I pray in many different ways. Besides kneeling and praying, I pray before I get out of bed. I pray throughout the day regardless of where I am.

**Be Quiet
Be Still
Be Silent
Before The
Lord**

I heard this saying, "Thank you, Lord, for helping me have a good day. Everything is going really good for me so far. I have not been angry or lost my temper. I have not felt any bitterness in my heart. Of course, I haven't gotten out of bed yet, but thank you." This saying puts a smile on my face.

I know God answers prayer as He has answered hundreds of my prayers. It is only if you are a Christian that you understand this statement. An unbeliever would say, *hundreds?* But this is a true statement when the center of your life is Christ.

We need quiet time with God. If you go to prayer with a short time span because you need to be off to work or get your children off to school, this is not *quiet time* before the Lord.

Find time every day to kneel before the Lord. Prayer draws us closer to God and can change the direction of our lives. Without a prayerful life, you are vulnerable to the darkness and sin of the world. When life's struggles come, you are not ready spiritually.

"Be still and know that I am God." (Ps. 46:10a) Be quiet before the Lord and let Him speak to you. Spend time in His presence. How can God speak to you if you are doing all the talking? He may be saying, "I have a new path for you to follow. The other path is no longer an option." Let God lead and guide you as He wants to show you new and wonderful things.

3. Praise

Praise is a very important part of prayer. As we give praise to God, we receive strength. Praise God every day for the good things in your life. When you are going through a difficult time, this is the *best time* to thank Him for his many blessings.

At the time you are in the middle of a crisis, this is when we may want to say, "Why, God? Why did this happen?" But once you start praising Him, you will feel the love of God sweep over you, and your fears and anxieties will begin to melt away.

Thank Him for your family and friends. Thank him for the beautiful weather, your comfortable home, and the blue bird singing. "Therefore, I will praise you among the nations, O Lord; I will sing praises to your name." (Ps. 18: 49)

My favorite verse for praise is Habakkuk 3:17–18.

> Though the fig tree does not bud
> And there are no grapes on the vines,
> Though the olive crop fails
> And the fields produce no food,
> Though there are no sheep in the pen
> And no cattle in the stalls,
> Yet I will rejoice in the Lord,
> I will be joyful in God my Savior.

This verse is telling us to take our thoughts off our present circumstances and praise God for what He is doing in our life. If there are no sheep in the pen we still praise Him!

I have found a wonderful tool for praising God. I have an old hymnal which has the most wonderful songs. I use it not necessarily to sing along, but I read the words as praise in my devotions.

Also, if I am singing a song, I will put my own name in it or the name of my son, such as there will be peace in the valley for Greg someday. I often will make up songs when I am driving. After all, no one else is hearing me except the Lord.

Praise God for His promises. Take time to read Psalms, and

you will learn how to praise our Lord and Savior. He deserves our praise!

**"Rejoice in the Lord always.
I will say it again: Rejoice!"
(Phil. 4:4)**

4. Church Attendance

There are two excuses people often use for not attending church. I have heard people say, "I do not feel I have to go to church to be a Christian." If we want to do God's will, the Bible tells us to meet together with other Christians and encourage one another. God wants to bless you through others and for you to also bless them.

While in church, God will speak to you through the message, through a song, or through another Christian friend. The pastor prays, asking God to give him a message to preach. When the pastor is speaking, God will speak to you. We all need to learn more about our Creator and grow spiritually through the pastor and teachers in our church.

Going to church can become a ritual, if you are not going for the right reasons. Church is a place we come and hear good music and meet new friends, but more importantly, church is where we come to worship. We attend church because we want to draw closer to Him. We want to learn of His plan for our lives.

The second excuse people will use is, "There are so many people in church who are hypocrites." They then begin to tell you a story of what happened in their church. It is good to remember no church is perfect as churches are full of people who are not perfect, people like you and me.

In every church, just as in any other setting where you have a group of people meeting together, there are going to be disagreements and challenges. There are people who will not agree with your opinions. There are people who do things wrong in your eyes. There are going to be people who disappoint you. We must keep our eyes on Jesus, not on others. They are not perfect and they fail us, but Jesus will never fail us.

Many go to church sitting near the back and leave quickly at the end of the service. This person could go to church for years, and no one would know them. They never become a part of the church family. If we love God, we want to serve God. It's important to have an active part in your church and get to know others so you can be of service in the building of God's kingdom.

Try different churches until you find the one you feel is right for you.

5. Associate with Other Christians

Most churches today have small groups you can join which meet once a week or you may find a Bible study group or Christian women's group in your area. This is where you can develop close relations with other Christians.

In this kind of setting, other Christians will pray with you, and they will also have their times of need, and you will have the blessing of praying with them.

Remember, the world is not centered on you and your problems. You can discipline yourselves to put your problems aside and think of others. Develop a passion to help other parents who have lost hope. Ask God to show you how you can be an encouragement to others.

Make a personal commitment to fellowship with other

Christians. Involve yourselves in the lives of others, and you will find lifelong friendships.

This may be a hard commitment for some as we often feel our week is already too busy. Where is your focus? Sometimes, it may take a crisis or a tragedy in life to make us slow down our lives. If we set our focus on things above, this will change how we live our lives each day and how we invest our time.

We always find time for fun and recreation. We find time for going to soccer games or the movies. We find time for most anything we really want to do. God wants to be the first priority in our lives. Misplaced priorities can cause us to look back at a wasted life. Let's not forget that this is not our home; heaven is our home.

Again, everything in life is not about us. The Bible tells us to associate with other Christians. This takes *ACTION* on our part to join a small group and be a blessing to others.

I am thankful for Christian friends. While going through stress and pain with our son, I needed to depend on the prayers of others. There were many Christians lifting us up in prayer.

Try different care groups or Bible study groups until you find the right one for you.

6. Witnessing

Now that is a scary word to some people. It has been said the one thing people are most afraid of is public speaking. Christians sometimes feel the same way about witnessing.

You do not need to be a great preacher to share the gospel effectively. We are all called to be disciples. Witnessing is actually easier than you may think. All it means is to talk to someone about God and what He has done for you. You can make a comment at meal time, saying, "I am really trusting God," or

"I thank God for friends who are helping me." Mention God to a friend or coworker in conversation.

We are planting a spiritual seed. Another Christian comes along and waters the seed. It is God who speaks to their hearts. It really is as simple as that. Talk about God to others and pray for them. In time, they may ask you questions and ask your opinion on godly things. They may begin to tell you a difficult time they are going through, which gives you an opportunity to witness to them.

If you look for opportunities, God will open doors for you to witness. Our pastor once asked, "Does everyone know you are a Christian at your work or school? Does everyone in your neighborhood know you are a Christian? Does everyone in your social circle know you are a Christian? If not, you have some witnessing to do."

God is not asking you to do something you are not capable of. He is asking you to take the first step toward witnessing. He is the one who speaks to the heart of that person.

If witnessing is easy for you, then push yourself even more. Get out of your comfort zone. God may put us in situations in which we have to stretch ourselves in what we think we are capable of doing. This is how we learn to depend on Him.

The Bible tells us to go into all the world and preach the gospel. It does not say, "Attention, all pastors, go into all the world and preach the gospel." God is talking to you and me. We are his disciples, and we are the ones who are to spread God's Word in *our world*.

There is a wonderful sign as I drive from my church parking lot. It says, "You are now entering the mission field." What is your mission field? Your mission field is everyone you know—family, acquaintances, coworkers, neighbors, your circle of friends, and the lady at the cash register.

We are not all missionaries. God may not be calling us to go to another country to spread the gospel, but He is calling us all to be His disciples.

There are opportunities for us to help others. You may find yourself in a group setting and sense someone is feeling left out. Go to them and be a friend. When you see the elderly man across the street having a difficult time mowing his lawn, volunteer to help him.

Give out kindness. You can send someone an encouraging message, make brownies to cheer someone up, and let someone else take the last parking space. It takes so little to put a smile on someone's face, and these are also ways of witnessing.

There are people who are broken and hurting and you can be sunshine to their souls. I am not forgetting that you, right now, are going through hard times of your own. This is why this is the best, the very best time, for you to reach out to others.

Take the focus off yourself and ask God, "What can I do for you today, Lord?" God has given each of us abilities that will strengthen the body of believers. Your special ability may seem small, but it is equally important to the kingdom of God. Develop your potential in God.

You will be amazed at the blessings you will receive. God's love heals our wounds so we can then show God's love to others. It is the sacrifice that will bring a wonderful blessing to you.

7. Finding a New Purpose

A Christian never retires. You may have retired from being a teacher or you may be planning to retire from being an accountant, but we never retire from being a Christian. It does not matter your age. God has so much more for you to do. He is not through with you yet.

The time you are given here on earth, however many years, this is *your individual lifetime.* What will you do with these years? Ask God for a new purpose in life. Listen to Him as He speaks to your heart.

Regardless of your age and regardless how long you have been a Christian; there is work for you to do in the kingdom of God. He will not ask more of you than you are capable of. Finding a new purpose will give you the opportunity to fill your heart and mind with something different than dwelling on your adult child.

A new purpose will take the focal point of your life off your son or daughter. It is also a healthy thing to stop talking about your own crisis to other people other than asking for prayer. Even our closest friends may get tired of hearing our woes. Don't you find that to be true? There is no question they care. God anxiously waits for us to come to Him with whatever is on our hearts.

What will you sacrifice in time? You have resources, talents, and abilities, but do you care enough? Can you teach a class at church for children? Can you sing in the choir? Can you visit the sick and the elderly? Can you lead a Bible study? Can you pass out bulletins?

Find a new purpose by doing something new and different with your time.

- Volunteer at the hospital.
- Visit those needing encouragement.
- Reorganize your kitchen.
- Begin a walking exercise.

- Meet your neighbors.
- Explore your local library.
- Learn a new language.
- Join a book club.
- Research your ancestors.
- Look up old friends on Facebook.
- Make a picture album for someone as a gift.
- Start a journal.

Replace hurt and grief with *ACTION*.

At the end of life I want to be able to say; "I have fought the good fight, I have finished the race, I have kept the faith. (2 Tim. 4:7)

**When life is over
Have I given my best?
Have I cared enough?
Have I been faithful?
Will He Say,
"Well Done?"**

If I asked you if you want to grow spiritually, most everyone will easily say yes. But do you really? Growing closer to the Lord takes *ACTION* on your part and the seven elements of spiritual growth can literally change your life.

The chart on the last page may seem like being in school again. However, if we honestly mark the chart each day, it will show us where we need to grow spiritually. Do you see the significance of the seven elements of spiritual growth? Are you spending enough time with God each day?

Step Three Action

These are the seven elements of spiritual growth that require commitment on your part. Start your Spiritual Growth plan today.

1. Reading God's Word
2. Prayer
3. Praise
4. Church Attendance
5. Associate with Other Christians
6. Witnessing
7. Finding a New Purpose

Fill out your chart at the end of each day for one month. I know God will bless you by doing this spiritual growth exercise!

I pray that through reading "When a Mother's Heart is Broken" you have received encouragement. Hopefully, you have found practical steps to change your present circumstances.

If you are grieving the loss of a child, thank God for the time He gave you with your son or daughter. This child was a wonderful gift. Remember them with joy but prayerfully finish grieving. He will give you the courage to go forward with your life.

You may be enduring the pain and suffering your adult child continues to send your way. Love them with your whole heart. Love them unconditionally. Never give up on them. Forgive them and forgive yourself, but it is time to *let go* of them and allow yourself to heal.

Most importantly; live a happy life regardless of your adult child's broken promises and rebellious lifestyle. God's love for you is beyond what you would ever be able to comprehend and because of that love He is asking you to *trust Him* with your adult child.

God's plan for you is not to live a life of stress and unhappiness, but an amazing and wonderful life of peace and joy.

My prayers are with you and may God bless you abundantly.

Seven Elements of Spiritual Growth Chart

	1	2	3	4	5	6	7	8	9	10	11	12	13	14	15
Reading Gods Word	X		X	X	X			X	X	X					
Prayer		X	X		X	X	X		X		X	X	X		
Praise		X			X					X	X			X	
Attend Church	X						X						X		
Associate with Other Christians	X					X	X						X		
Witness			X					X	X		X			X	
Find a New Purpose	X					X	X					X			

Seven Elements of Spiritual Growth Chart

	16	17	18	19	20	21	22	23	24	25	26	27	28	29	30	31
Reading Gods Word				X		X	X	X			X					
Prayer				X	X	X			X		X	X				
Praise		X	X			X				X			X	X		
Attend Church								X						X		
Associate with Other Christians			X								X	X		X		
Witness					X	X			X				X		X	
Find a New Purpose				X							X			X		

Seven Elements of Spiritual Growth

	1	2	3	4	5	6	7	8	9	10	11	12	13	14	15
Reading Gods Word															
Prayer															
Praise															
Attend Church															
Associate with Other Christians															
Witness															
Find a New Purpose															

Seven Elements of Spiritual Growth

	16	17	18	19	20	21	22	23	24	25	26	27	28	29	30	31
Reading Gods Word																
Prayer																
Praise																
Attend Church																
Associate with Other Christians																
Witness																
Find a New Purpose																

Notes

1. *Humpty Dumpty* written by Lewis Carroll in 1810 as a poem
2. *Doing Time - Life Inside the Big House* - 1991 documentary film directed by Alan Raymond
3. *Dog Day Afternoon* – Film made in 1975 directed by Sidney Lumet and screenplay by Frank Pierson
4. *What a Friend we have in Jesus* - music by Charles C. Converse 1868 - public domain
5. *Standin in the Need of Prayer* - Composed by Hank Cockran
6. *Farther Along* – written by W.B. Stevens - public domain
7. *Old Rugged Cross* – written by George Bennard – public domain
8. *God's Loan* – poem written by Edgar Guest in 1949